Praise for

EVERYONE BUT MYSELF

"Wise and hilarious, Chavez had me rooting for her from page one. Her story will be a hopeful beacon to anyone standing on shaky ground."
—CHRISTIE TATE, author of *Group*

"Brilliantly, Chavez portrays the pressures and pitfalls of twenty-first-century motherhood. I read this book in one fell swoop, gasping with recognition on every single page, and finishing with the wonderful feeling that I was not alone in the world."
—JOANNA RAKOFF, author of *My Salinger Year*

"If you find yourself overwhelmed and teetering on the edge (like most of us): don't panic. Take a deep breath . . . Julie Chavez (your new best friend) will help you find solid ground in this funny and heartwarming memoir."
—JEN MANN, author of *Midlife Bites:
Anyone Else Falling Apart, or Is It Just Me?*

"Hilarious. Poignant. Overall awesome. This is one of those books that we know our fellow moms out there will be obsessed with."
—CAT & NAT, coauthors of *Mom Secrets* and *Mom Truths*

"I can't remember the last time I read a book with so much heart. Every page is full of love—love for the life she's built, one that seems in danger of disappearing as she struggles with her mental health. Hers is an honest, painful, cautionary tale for any woman who thinks self-sacrifice will make you a better partner and parent."
—KRISTIN VAN OGTROP, author of *Did I Say That Out
Loud?: Midlife Indignities and How to Survive Them*

"Everything about Chavez's story of managing motherhood, work, marriage, anxiety . . . spoke to me. Her fresh, honest, hilarious voice makes her so relatable. The perfect memoir for any mom who feels pulled in a million directions."
—JILL SMOKLER, author of *Confessions of a Scary Mommy* and
founder of Scary Mommy and She's Got Issues

"A balm for the working mother and for caregivers of all kinds. With tenderness, warmth, and an attentive eye, Chavez documents the journey of a woman learning to belong to herself."

—ABBY MASLIN, author of *Love You Hard: A Memoir of Marriage, Brain Injury, and Reinventing Love*

"When you are used to giving to others but saving nothing for yourself, the sense of depletion is so strong it's hard to make changes. In this thoughtful, gentle memoir, Chavez shows how she began to choose herself and, little by little, regain hope and purpose."

—ANNA WHISTON-DONALDSON, author of *Rare Bird: A Memoir of Loss and Love*

"[Chavez] finds her way back to mental health and joyfulness in this candid and deeply heartfelt memoir that will resonate with any reader who has struggled to be all that the world asks."

—COURTNEY MAUM, author of *The Year of the Horses: A Memoir*

"In this beautifully written and brutally honest memoir . . . we walk away with a renewed ability to accept our frailty, leading us to a place of self-kindness, mindfulness, and common humanity."

—STEPHANIE THORNTON PLYMALE, author of *American Daughter: A Memoir*

"Chavez's book gently—and sometimes not-so-gently—suggests that finding the words to ask for mental health help isn't the hardest part, that it's actually acknowledging the roadblocks we've been taught to just push through. Her journey is a vulnerable one, yes, but also bitingly funny and incredibly relatable. What a gift."

—KEELY FLYNN, columnist and humorist for *Chicago Parent* magazine

EVERYONE BUT MYSELF

a memoir

Julie Chavez

ZIBBY BOOKS
NEW YORK

Everyone But Myself: A Memoir

Copyright © 2024 by Julie Chavez

All rights reserved. No part of this book may be used, reproduced, distributed, or transmitted in any form or by any means without the prior written permission of the publisher, except as permitted by U.S. copyright law. Published in the United States by Zibby Books, New York.

Zibby Books, colophon, and associated logos are trademarks and/or registered trademarks of Zibby Media LLC.

The author has tried to re-create events, locales, and conversations based on their own memories and those of others. In some instances, in order to maintain their anonymity, certain names, characteristics, and locations have been changed.

Excerpt from GIFT FROM THE SEA by Anne Morrow Lindbergh, copyright © 1955, 1975, copyright renewed 1983 by Anne Morrow Lindbergh. Used by permission of Pantheon Books, an imprint of the Knopf Doubleday Publishing Group, a division of Penguin Random House LLC. All rights reserved.

THE BODY KEEPS THE SCORE by Bessel van der Kolk, M.D.. Used by permission of Penguin Random House LLC.

Library of Congress Control Number: 2023934635
Paperback ISBN: 978-1-958506-05-9
Hardcover ISBN: 979-8-9852828-4-9
eBook ISBN: 979-8-9862418-6-9

Book design by Neuwirth & Associates
Cover design by Graça Tito
www.zibbymedia.com

Printed in the United States of America
10 9 8 7 6 5 4 3 2 1

To Amy, who never doubted I could

A NOTE TO THE READER

"Mrs. Chavez, what's this book about?"
The question sails across the library in a distinctly non-library voice, a volume knob set to seven when it should be at two. My third-grade students mill about the stacks: checking the shelves, comparing choices with their friends, whispering the alphabet to locate the right call number, running their hands along the colorful spines. The voice belongs to Adam, a dark-haired boy who, when he was in kindergarten, knew more about the solar system than I did. Above all those heads, I raise my finger to my lips and give a pointed, mildly exasperated look, a reminder about not shouting in the library.

I walk over to Adam to answer his question. It's a question that, even for a librarian, isn't always easy to answer: What is this story about?

Outside of nonfiction that's devoted to a concrete topic—anatomy or Mars or how the Golden Gate Bridge came to be painted international orange—some of my favorite books are *about* so much more than their plots.

If you ask me about my favorite books, you may not immediately see a common thread in their topics or even their format. I have adored memoirs and children's picture books, have treasured novels and short stories. But the books that stay with me do have commonality, for they're stories that extract meaning from the mundane. These books echo my own deep desire to see miracles and joy hidden among the laundry and the driving and the same, tired arguments that I have with my husband. These books remind me to cling to what's good, to live a life that's full and present.

(It's challenging to explain this to a third-grader, but I try to get the point across.)

In the case of this book, the one you're reading now, I know what it's about. If I were standing with you in the library, I would place it in your hands and tell you that this is the story of a time in which I stopped caring for myself, a season in which I felt so pressed for minutes, so pummeled by the needs of the people I loved, that the only logical option—for a perfectionist, that is— was to relinquish the space I'd previously marked for myself and instead devote it to doing, accomplishing, checking off the small, tidy boxes on an endless to-do list.

This book is about the consequences of that self-neglect. For me, the result was anxiety, depression, and an obfuscation of the habits and practices that provided sustenance, rest, and joy. I was lost inside my own beautiful life.

Although the details vary, I'm not alone in this story. Many women ask the same questions I did: How do I respond to all the asks of the world without losing my sense of self—my interests, my desires, my dreams—in the process? How do I remain whole so that, underneath all the repetitive and the annoying and the boring, I can revel in the privilege and miracle of a perfectly messy life?

I continue to hear a low hum of conversation as I walk over to Adam, quiet exclamations of "That one was so good!" and "Have you read this one?" I take the book out of his hand and consider the cover before I deliver my answer.

"Buddy, I haven't yet read this one, but I'd bet there's something in there for you. Read it and let me know." I put the book back in his hands and send him off to scan it at the circulation desk. Unlike some of my less enthusiastic readers, I'm confident Adam will actually open the book. I smile at the thought of his little hands cracking that spine, of the two of us discussing the story's finer points after he's finished.

Friend, I hope this book holds something for you too. Read it and let me know.

1

I N THE MOMENT IT'S HAPPENING, a panic attack can convince you of nearly anything.

That night, I believed there was a very real possibility I would die, even though I was safe inside my home in Northern California, my two healthy boys sleeping just down the hall. My husband, Mando, was in Dallas, doing the work of a twenty-first-century traveling salesman for a large winery. I'd taken a shower, hoping to calm myself, but it hadn't worked.

I was thirty-eight years old, and I was scared to turn off the lights.

I paused in the doorway between my bathroom and bedroom: face scrubbed clean, teeth brushed, wet hair dampening my pajama T-shirt. My left hand rested on the bathroom light switch, but I was too frightened to flip it and plunge the room into darkness. I hesitated for another long moment before giving up and leaving it on. I stepped across the room, the wood floor creaking below my feet, the halogen bulbs from the vanity still lighting the space at a brightness I'd typically deem intolerable for sleep. I pulled aside the fluffy duvet in its white cover; I parted the cool sheets and shakily arranged my pillows. I completed all these small, methodical movements that marked the close of another day while I tried desperately to get a grip.

My heart thumped violently in my rib cage. My breath came in short, shallow spurts. I tried to lengthen the inhales, to take a full, smooth breath, but succeeded only in chaining them together: *shoo-shoo-shoo*. I was trying to soothe myself just as I had soothed the boys when they were small, nearly including the gentle bounce that becomes second nature to most new parents, lodging so deeply inside us that my mom once found herself bouncing a plastic baby doll.

Tears made tracks down my cheeks as I tucked myself into my side of the king bed I shared with my husband of sixteen years. I was alone. I put my hand on my chest, using the pressure to try to smooth the breaths from the outside. I tried to convince myself I wasn't dying.

My two sons slept in their rooms just across the hall, so close that I heard one of them shift in his bed. I could picture the outline of their sleeping bodies. Nolan was eleven. Conscientious and precocious, a child who loved nothing more than to obliterate a comfortable silence, he always slept on his stomach with his head turned to the right, his hands nestled underneath his pillow. Eli was nine and slept on his side, legs tucked up, one arm likely dangling over the edge of the bed. The glasses he'd worn since age two were placed on his shelf next to his latest LEGO creation, a mug full of his favorite pens, and an odd-shaped clay duck he made in kindergarten. Eli was fun, easygoing, and occasionally overconfident, the yin to his brother's yang. My husband and I orbited around them, these two suns that anchored our galaxy.

I attempted to calm myself by considering the boys, their bodies peaceful and at rest. I tried in vain to ground myself in the familiar noises of our home, but instead, I flinched at the sounds that typically comforted me, like the gentle clicking of the leaves of the birch tree that grew just outside our bedroom window.

I monitored my breathing, watching for signs of a major allergic reaction to something invisible in my environment. Was my body releasing the flood of inflammatory chemicals that could trigger the cascade into respiratory distress? Was my breathing shallow because I was afraid? Or was it something physiological that was shortening my inhales? More tears. *Shoo-shoo-shoo*, the breaths interspersed with hitches of sobs. I tried to quiet my crying so I could listen for wheezing. Would the boys know what to do? Whose number would they dial if I were unresponsive? I had prepared them for stranger danger, the nondescript white van with promised puppies behind its sliding door. I had taught them not to touch the stove. They knew better than to run into the street. But in all my efforts to equip them, I had never imagined the scenario of their mother dying in the middle of the night while their father was on a business trip.

That thought sent me into more spasms of fear.

I didn't call Mando. The time difference meant he was already asleep; he had an early-morning meeting, and I knew he had silenced his phone in an attempt to find a healthy stretch of rest in the unfamiliar hotel bed. We were married at twenty-two and he was the love of my life, which is to say he was both my best friend and a maddening roommate with whom I once had a daylong argument about shoes being placed on the shoe rack (instead of next to the shoe rack). Through the ups and downs of nearly two decades, Mando was one of the cornerstones of my life. But I didn't pick up the phone to dial him.

My panic convinced me that reaching out was useless. How could I have explained what was happening when even I didn't fully understand what was happening? I made no calls: not to my parents, who lived in Japan for my father's work and were already in the early evening of the following day due to the time difference; not to my sister, Amy, who lived in Austin and would have picked up on the second ring; not to my friend Cathie, who lived only two streets away with her husband, a former paramedic; not to my best friend, Allie, who lived two streets away in the other direction. My phone lay impotent and undisturbed on the nightstand beside me, next to the ever-present stack of books and a small blue alarm clock.

I lay in bed with Mando's pillows propped up behind me, imagining his body there beside me. The lights stayed on as I curled myself into a tight ball, whispering a mantra to myself, my voice shaking. "You're okay, you're okay, you're okay." I said it over and over—"you're okay, you're okay, you're okay." But I couldn't quite make myself believe it.

2

I N MY EXPERIENCE, THE PHRASE *all of a sudden* is rarely applicable to mental health.

My panic attack that night sprouted from a specific fear: I would die of anaphylaxis, the worst-case-scenario end of any severe allergic reaction. It was a fear that had been slowly growing for five months, its roots snaking and looping until it burst through the surface, no longer containable.

The previous fall, the boys and I had been receiving regular allergy shots after a scratch test revealed that we all reacted to nearly everything except food: dust, mold, cats, dogs, trees, flowers, grass. With each round of titrated injections, we were exposed to an increased dose of our specific allergens. This gradual process recalibrates the immune system so that eventually the body no longer responds to the allergen as a threat.

The shots we received on one warm, Friday November morning were unremarkable: three injections for each of us. The boys and I finished our required thirty-minute waiting period in the office and then went to In-N-Out, soaking up sunshine and drinking our milkshakes.

But on the way home, my scalp started to itch, followed by my ears. I parked the car in the garage, rushed through the door, and walked straight to the hall mirror. I pulled up the edge of my T-shirt sleeve to examine my injection site, having been told that a typical, acceptable skin reaction would be about the size of a dime. As I turned my body to view my left triceps, I saw an angry, red, splotchy area the size of a handprint. I found my phone and dialed the doctor's office; I listened to the clicking computer sounds as the nurse pulled up my chart. There was a pause and she responded, almost casually, "Well, why don't you come back in, and we'll have a look." I took a deep shaking breath and called Mando, who was mercifully on his way home from the local office. I had no way of anticipating that I'd want him beside me over the next few hours, and so we employed our customary divide-and-conquer approach: the boys waited for him at home while I sped back to the doctor's office. By the time I arrived ten minutes later, my lips were itching, and I was starting to wheeze.

The nurse examined me and then called the physician assistant, who listened to my lungs. After she finished, the PA looped the stethoscope around her neck, moving her curly hair out of the way. She instructed the nurse to give me a shot of epinephrine before leaving to see her other patients. After receiving the injection in the leg, I zipped up my jeans and sat on the edge of the table, trying to calm myself.

I watched the nurse pop the used syringe into the red sharps disposal container mounted on the wall and deftly remove her purple gloves, discarding them in the trash as she turned to note the time of the injection on a small piece of paper.

"You're going to feel like you've had about eighteen cups of coffee," she said in a well-rehearsed tone, kind but distant. "Let me know if you start feeling itchy again. I'll be back to check on you." She filled a flowered Dixie cup with water and left the room to go administer more routine shots.

I waited on the table as the epinephrine rushed through my arteries to counteract my body's response to the original shot, my heart rate soaring and my body shaking. The heat and itching stopped their slow build and then subsided, but the feeling of helplessness remained, overwhelming me. I had no plan, no details, no understanding of outcomes or progress in this situation. No information had been offered to me. I didn't leave the room to find someone who could tell me what was happening. I waited, just as I'd been told to.

Twenty minutes later, the nurse popped her head back into the room to check in. I told her I thought my ears were starting to itch again. They were feeling hot to me. I held back my additional questions, working to hide my mounting panic, to suggest that I still had everything under control.

"Do you have eczema there?"

She spoke kindly, and yet it was clear that she wasn't concerned. As she rubbed cream on my ears, her gloves tapping the ointment gently onto my cartilage, I couldn't shake the feeling that she was placating me. I was suddenly awash in self-doubt.

Was I itching, or was I overreacting? Was my chest tight because I was wheezing or because I was weighted down by fear? Was I foolish to feel this terrified when her every move telegraphed that this was a standard, everyday situation?

And so I lay on the table, waiting for her to come back, waiting for the PA to come back, lying under an air-conditioning vent set to arctic. It was freezing in the tiny room.

My lips started to itch again.

This time I was sure, but still, I waited for her return like an obedient, terrified, almost–middle-aged patient.

The nurse returned and quickly summoned the PA, who ordered another shot of epinephrine in addition to a dose of prednisone, a commonly used steroid. And that's when I lost my shit. I started to sob. What if they couldn't stop this? The allergen was there, flowing through my blood, and my body was not having it. I felt a complete loss of control.

Just as I was thinking these terrible, frightening thoughts, my body started processing the second shot of adrenaline. Though it provided my body what it needed to fight down the allergic reaction, it had the side effect of putting my brain into *orbit*. All I could think of was dying, of being torn from my husband, my precious children, my sweet life. I whispered a prayer to calm myself, but it didn't work. I curled up in the fetal position in the cold room and wept, soaking the paper sheet on the exam table. The nurse brought me a flimsy blanket, and then I was alone.

Time passed, and I started to come back down. I shivered from the chill in the cold room, from the inadequacy of the flip-flops and thin hoodie I had chosen for the warm California day, and from the surplus of adrenaline in my system. I shook because

I had been shaken, deeply, in ways I wouldn't fully understand for a long time to come.

Traumas—even small traumas, the sort one might not even refer to as a trauma for fear of sounding overly dramatic—don't always dissipate. They lay in wait.

3

THE PUNCTURE OF THAT ALLERGY shot needle in November introduced a tiny leak, nearly imperceptible at first. I didn't hear the slightly audible hiss of air over those intervening months. I was busy, busy, busy: as moms are, as caregivers are, as parents with a traveling partner are. I was the woman who dropped off the snacks, who volunteered for the field trip, who regularly wolfed down cereal over the sink for lunch and ate a Clif Bar for dinner in the car. The ticker tape in my brain ticked at a steady clip from first thing in the morning until I washed my face and flossed my teeth at night. But as I ran about being oh-so-busy, the puncture tore, little by little.

A few hours before The Night I Couldn't Turn Off the Lights, it started to rip.

On that late afternoon in April, when I found my seat in the bleachers at Nolan's baseball game, I didn't initially notice that the Bradford pear trees above my head were raining blossoms, their branches whipping in the sharp, early-evening wind.

Instead, I was busy keeping score. When the coach had asked for a scorekeeper at the beginning of the season, I'd volunteered, not realizing that baseball scorekeeping would mean I could forget about watching my child play. My job was to meticulously track the details of the game, full stop.

I'd raised my hand because volunteering—showing up, helping out, making life easy, paying close attention—was one of the many ways I scored myself on my all-consuming mission to be a Good Mom.

I pulled out two of the sharpened pencils that lived inside my luxurious Tory Burch bag, mucking up the gorgeous pockets with a series of tiny lead hashes, like prisoners marking the days. The bag, a gift from Mando, was once pristine and organized but had slowly descended into chaos, becoming merely a vessel to collect the detritus of life.

Eli stepped up onto the bleachers before dropping heavily beside me.

"Mom, do you have money?"

"I don't know," I said, distracted, one of the pencils already scratching against the paper. "Check my wallet." He pawed through my purse as I copied the afternoon's batting lineup.

Eli emerged from my bag with a five-dollar bill. The bag's leather bottom scraped on the fiberglass as he pushed it back toward me.

"I'm gonna go get a hot dog," he said, and bounced away. I batted down the usual fears that sprung up reflexively, like a game of anxiety Whac-A-Mole I had no choice but to play all day, every day.

Hot dogs are a choking hazard: *whack*. If I were a kidnapper, I would case a sports park: *whack*. Eli got lost that one time on his scooter: *whack*.

I shook myself out of it and continued filling in details on the giant scorebook spread across my lap. We were the home team, which meant we pitched first. I marked down the short lines to keep track of the pitch count. That was the easy part. When we were up to bat, I filled in strikes, balls, hits. Did the batter strike out looking? A fly ball? To what side of the outfield? Did anyone score? Was it a single or a double, and was it the result of a hit or an error by the clueless kid manning second base? I marked as quickly as I could, quietly cursing myself for not watching the twenty-minute YouTube tutorial on scorekeeping.

I occasionally turned to my neighbor for backup. "Hey, who just batted?" I asked.

"Number seven."

"Damn," I hissed under my breath. "I missed someone." And then, audibly, chirpily, Stepford-wifely added, "Okay, thanks!"

I couldn't help but question why I'd signed up for this job in the first place. Sure, I'd wanted to be helpful, but how had I ignored the obvious fact that I was ill equipped for this particular role? I knew a lot about volleyball, a fair amount about football, and nothing about baseball. During the previous season Mando had told me multiple times that shouting "catch it catch it catch it" was "not helpful."

Baseball scorekeeping records everything. It's complex, and there's always more that can be recorded, more that can be done. It's less like counting and more like advanced statistics (I was capable of the former and awful at the latter). But I couldn't quit. I couldn't quit anything. Let down the coach, the team, my children? It simply wasn't an option. I hated quitting more than I hated advanced statistics.

The early-spring blossoms continued to fall around the sports park as I scribbled frantically in the book. I occasionally set down the pencil to flex my cold, stiff fingers. The sun dropped below the ridge to the west and the wind whipped across the fields in mean, icy gusts.

Eli came back, ketchup on his chin, safe and sound. Crisis (crises) averted.

But as he sat back down next to me, my eyes began to itch. I grabbed at tissues between batters. A new potential crisis took shape. Panic slithered its way through the small opening created by these completely normal symptoms to whisper, *You should have never started those shots. Now your allergies could kill you. It'll be like it was at the doctor's office—but you're here, in the middle of a baseball game, and nobody can save you in time.*

Though it had begun with a tiny pinprick, that trauma in November had waited, poised to strike. It seized its moment at the game. Later that night, when I found myself too scared to turn off the lights, it attacked ferociously at my most fervent desire: to control what happens in my life.

4

I SAT IN FRONT OF the students on the morning after my panic attack. My heart raced as I read to them from *Chrysanthemum*, a Kevin Henkes book that requires a sassy, singsong voice for the character of Victoria, because Victoria is a brat.

The wooden chair beneath me creaked slightly as I recrossed my legs, shifting the book to my left hand. As the children sat before me on the rainbow carpet, my entire body trembled, prickling with nervous energy, the visceral aftershocks of last night's fear creating a low, steady electric current just beneath my skin. I was heavy with tiredness, chilled even though the day was warm. But I kept reading.

I've always wished my library had windows, but on the morning after The Night I Couldn't Turn Off the Lights, I didn't notice their absence. I was trapped inside my own head, trying to sort out what had happened to me—and there were no windows in there, either.

· · ·

The elementary school library where I spend my days sits in the center of two wings of classrooms, a large space at the middle of the school that serves as a shortcut and a connector. When you walk into my library, you'll notice that I've done everything possible to compensate for the lack of natural light, to distract your eye from the sickly hospital green that was chosen as the color for the cabinets, to soften the headache-inducing fluorescent lighting. It's a children's library, for goodness' sake. The word to describe the ambience shouldn't be *industrial*.

When I took the job in 2018, it was someone else's recently vacated space, like a new apartment that held the lingering traces of its former occupants, replete with unfamiliar scents and mysterious stains on the carpet whose origins could only be guessed at (or catastrophized). Since the library is quite large, I was still finding time to catalog its contents. There were cabinets that remained a mystery, binders with details from the early 2000s, and stuffed animals that I was convinced were housing entire cities of dust mites and would therefore have to be eliminated.

I began by adding twinkle lights when I was in my second year on the job, teetering barefoot on a ladder to install hooks between the tiles of the fifteen-foot ceilings. I hung them haphazardly, looping the wires above the carpet where the students sit crisscross applesauce for read-alouds. The rug's colored rows are divided into thirty equally sized squares, though we often call them houses (as in "stay in your house, friend").

In my third year, I brought in large canvas prints of European cities to place above the nonfiction section, but it was in the fall of 2019, when I purchased a Cricut and my sister came to visit for a weekend, that the situation escalated. Amy and I spent a manic two days covering the ends of the shelving units with large color blocks of painstakingly applied Con-Tact paper, a process that included a quilter's rule and an X-Acto knife. The two of us smoothed out bubbles as we stuck and peeled and reapplied.

The next additions were a Harry Potter display with a Nimbus 2000 hanging from fishing wire, a book with paper butterflies flying out of its pages, and another set of twinkle lights—blue, this time, set against paper that looks like ocean water. I added three more rugs—two kelly green, one royal blue—and color-coordinated seating areas with miniature chairs and couches. The kids check out their books and then park themselves on the bright vinyl as if they're relaxing in a hip coffee shop.

I'm fortunate to have plenty of shelf space and, at last count, more than sixteen thousand titles. There are small subsections for graphic novels and biographies, and picture books have a home in the small horseshoe around the rainbow carpet so the kindergarteners can be corralled, limiting their considerable potential for damage. Today, in my sixth year, I can confidently say it's my library. I know every nook and cranny.

But what brought me to the library wasn't the space—it was my boys. And, of course, the books.

When the boys started school, I looked for ways to be part of their universes, the simplest of which was volunteering. Through their early years I stapled, counted, and sorted my way into their school worlds, storing these brief glimpses of their lives away from me, all with the goal of understanding them better. If children are books to be read and not books to be written, then I was studying mine, researching them, combing the footnotes for the information that would make me a wiser, better mother.

This idea of what would make me a "better" mother was, as it is for many, closely tied to my availability. We often speak of "good" parents by measuring presence: he shows up for events; she attends all his baseball games; they chaperone field trips. We employ similar language for friendships and other relationships: *I'm here for you.* We can all point to the parents who are overstepping, living vicariously through their children, over-identifying with their successes and failures, but the vast majority of parents I know are shooting for the reasonable middle ground: the present, solid, dependable parent who cheers from the sidelines but isn't so emotionally invested that the other spectators cringe.

If I stayed close to my children—if I spoke their language, viewed the horizon from their perspectives, understood the context for their immature worldviews—I believed I could guide them along the right paths. And as a guide, I felt it incumbent upon me to pay close attention to the route that would usher them into the future we all desire for our children: happiness, health, joy.

I started off as a lunch recess supervisor. I walked the playground beat, sweating as I traversed the expanse of hot asphalt for two hours, three days a week. Seeing my kids at their new school gave me perspective on my boys and helped me know their classmates and the school staff. By opening tricky packaging for first-graders and refereeing kickball and mediating petty disputes, I believed I'd make my boys feel loved. They'd feel the unspoken message: I'm *here* for you.

One afternoon, the librarian, who happened to be the father

of one of Nolan's friends, stopped me on my way out the door to tell me he was hoping to move into another position at the school. He thought I should apply for his current job.

I initially dismissed it as too much, thinking that the nearly full-time hours and commitment would upset our family's carefully balanced apple cart. But the job was tailor-made for a book-lover like me, a person who purchased *Library Lion* after being so utterly charmed by the copy Nolan brought home from the library that she couldn't help herself. Perhaps it would be a room of my own, a quiet cocoon of control that would usher me into the next season of life. And Mando and I both agreed we could use the extra income. Moving to California had been a financial stretch. So, after further encouragement from the principal, Shay, whom I adored, and much discussion with Mando, I figured we could make it work. Being just down the hall from the boys would allow me to work and ensure my continued availability. And I loved books, after all. I thought I could help the children love them too.

I glanced up at one of the children and gave a subtle signal to him to stop picking his nose, adding a slight shake of my head, never breaking pace in my recitation of the familiar words. I was entirely disconnected from the act of reading *Chrysanthemum*, a performance done completely on autopilot. Victoria was about to get her comeuppance, a part of the book that typically filled my justice-loving heart with glee. But not this time.

My brain was preoccupied by a puzzle it couldn't solve.

Earlier that morning, before coming into work but after the boys had pedaled away to school on the neighborhood path that led directly to the back gate of the school, I had called the nurse at the allergy clinic. I stood in the kitchen, waiting for the phone to connect, the smooth surface of my phone case slippery in my shaky, sweaty hand. When the nurse came on the line, I ran her through the events: the baseball game, my very typical allergic reaction, the mitigation steps I'd taken when I'd arrived home.

"I just started to think I had maybe messed up my system with the shots," I had tried to explain to her. "Like maybe now I've oversensitized myself to the things I'm allergic to and now if I'm exposed to them in regular life I'll have another anaphylactic reaction?" I handed her the pieces, hoping she could make sense of the puzzle for me. But I didn't give her all the details. I didn't tell her I was scared of dying, or that I slept with the lights on. I told her what I could, and I waited for her to say the words that would free me, the words that would push back the adrenaline and terror and a deep sadness that was now loose inside me.

"That's never going to happen," she said. "The shot you had, the one you reacted to, had a concentrated dose that you'd never encounter in everyday life."

She'd offered the right words, and I had tried desperately to absorb them—but they'd done nothing for me. I'd known this already, on one level. So if I understood, why had the fear of death hijacked my brain?

She reassured me with science—with *facts*—about five more times before concluding our call.

After we hung up, I took a deep, shaky breath. I said it out loud to myself: "It's *never* going to happen." But my body continued to hum. I stood for a brief moment in the kitchen, pressing my hands against the countertop, pulling my shoulders back and down, straightening my spine. I tried to tell my body that it was done, that me, my body and I, we were okay.

The puzzle pieces had been laid out in front of me:

I had the systemic reaction to the allergy shot in November, which might very well have led to anaphylaxis if I hadn't received treatment.

I experienced a typical allergic reaction to the pollen in the trees.

I was concerned that this minor allergic response would lead to anaphylaxis, despite being assured by a medical professional that it would not.

If all these pieces fit, then why couldn't my brain assemble them? Why, despite everything being okay, did I still feel edgy and wired?

I gathered up my things and pedaled to school, because I can ride to work on my white bike with the basket, a commute as idyllic as if I lived on the set of *The Truman Show*.

But on that day I hadn't enjoyed its magic, because the mowers from the city were out in the greenbelt and the smell of fresh-cut grass made me want to weep with fear.

When I reached the final pages of *Chrysanthemum*, I didn't feel the surge of righteousness when Victoria forgets her lines in the school play, proving that what goes around comes around. My thoughts spun and roiled, and I functioned on only the tiniest sliver of mental energy, my anxiety demanding the rest.

I continued to give myself basic instructions: turn the page; turn the page; close the book; stand up; answer the question; scan the book; tell the child to sit down and stop yanking the pages.

I couldn't settle into any moment. Anxiety felt like helium, lifting me out of the present. I was a balloon, drifting over everything: the rainbow carpet, the dust mite–infested stuffed animals I had yet to feel okay about discarding, the students moving like busy ants below me. My physical body took up space, but I wasn't really there. The anxiety pumped and the helium whooshed, a steady slipstream of doubt, of what-ifs, of worst-case scenarios. *I could have inhaled some of that fresh-cut grass this morning. What if Nolan or Eli chokes on his lunch at school and no one knows the Heimlich maneuver? Could the small infection on the cuticle of my left ring finger be flesh-eating bacteria?*

Worst of all, I sensed that the string tying me down wasn't as secure as I'd previously believed. I needed someone or something to tether me, to attach me to the wooden chair I'd pulled over from one of the adult-size tables in the library, to tie a double knot and close the valve to the tank so the helium would stop pumping, so the adrenaline would stop lifting me out of my body.

Otherwise, what would prevent me from floating away?

5

My sister, Amy, is nearly ten years my junior, a surprise pregnancy for my parents on the week my mom registered my brother, Brian, for kindergarten in Denver, Colorado. When Amy was four months old, we moved to Eagle-Vail, so that my dad could open a new Hyatt property in Beaver Creek, a swanky ski resort just west of Vail. She began as a colicky baby and grew into a towheaded spitfire of a toddler who would hold me as a cuddling hostage, wrapping her skinny arm tightly around my neck so she could play with my hair.

The hotel business is one of transfers and moves, and my dad's job took my parents to Hilton Head, South Carolina, just before my senior year of high school. I lived with another family to finish out my final year—an act of love on my parents' part that I'm only now starting to fully grasp, as my own sons approach that seminal year, that momentous collection of last times.

In Hilton Head, my family lived in an apartment on the ninth floor of the hotel. Amy was a real-life Eloise, doted on by the staff and making mischief wherever possible. Everyone loved her.

Despite the age difference, we've managed to grow up together, sharing the peculiar mix of genetics, memory, history, and idiosyncrasy that binds us as family. Amy knows me. She knows, for example, that going to Disneyland turns me into a maximizing lunatic who feels compelled to determine the best plan for the day, hit all the best rides, and efficiently collect the appropriate FastPasses. If I mow down a few toddlers in pursuit of these goals, then so be it.

"Maximum fun!" shouts Disneyland Julie, in a voice a shade away from unhinged, exhorting her family to hurry up. We were once abandoned by friends in the park when they realized that our Disney pace is just short of an all-out sprint.

Amy knows who Disneyland Julie is.

And so she was fully aware, as we power-walked to the Cars ride in California Adventure, the FastPasses in her hand as I managed the stroller (with the child that was too big for the stroller because Disneyland Julie can't wait for these kids to just *walk*), that she'd be pushing me over the edge when she turned to me and said, at 11:14 a.m., "Julie, these passes were from ten to eleven, not eleven to twelve."

I stopped dead in the middle of the wide walkway, just in front of the Radiator Springs sign. "*What*." I stared at her in horror.

Amy's face broke into a satisfied, triumphant grin. "Just kidding," she managed to say, before laughing uncontrollably.

And that's why, on that cool January day at Disneyland, as she wiped tears of laughter from behind her glasses, I turned to

Amy—my soul sister, who happens to be my real sister—and I called her a fucker.

I didn't need to dodge or hide with Amy. I tapped her name to dial her number as I folded laundry after school, while the boys were busy with homework.

"I'm feeling weird," I said. "Like I can't turn off or something."

"That sounds like anxiety," Amy replied carefully, drawing from her own experience.

"Well, it's horrible."

"Have you talked to Mando?"

"Not yet. He has two more nights in Dallas." I couldn't stay on the phone for long. I had to check homework and make dinner and finish the laundry, because Nolan had only one pair of baseball pants, and there were often games on consecutive nights.

And really, what more was there to say? Was this anxiety? I couldn't yet find words that would adequately capture what I was experiencing. Nothing sounded quite right because nothing felt quite right.

"Okay, well, call me if you need me," she instructed. "Hang in there, sissy."

On that day, Amy gave me a name for my new worst friend: anxiety. And beginning with this phone call from the laundry room, my little sister became my primary touchstone. Over the coming months, she would answer every call, every text. She knew how much I needed her. Amy was the one to tether me through this time. She took the string of my balloon out of my shaking fingers and said, over and over, "I'll hold this for you."

6

When Mando returned from Dallas on Thursday, he walked in the door and enfolded me in his arms. I rested my head on his shoulder and took in the familiar, comforting scent of his collar, of the man I'd loved for more than half my life. I missed him terribly when he was gone, and I was thankful to know he missed us too.

"I'm so glad you're home. I love you."

"Me too," he said with an exhale, his eyes tired. "That flight was brutal. You guys doing okay?"

After he had unpacked—a process that took only a few short minutes because of his expert systems—I told him that I freaked out while he was gone. Those were the comically inadequate words I chose: I freaked out. I gave him the summary of events and then a summary of the call with the nurse. Like many parents, Mando and I often conversed in the language of Summaries, a pidgin developed for those short on time and patience, exceedingly useful for the overcommitted and for volunteer scorekeepers who can't talk during the game.

A fuller description of what I'd experienced on The Night I Couldn't Turn Off the Lights remained inaccessible to me. I could offer only this to Mando: I freaked out.

Anyway, there wasn't time to explain further. Eli had a game. Life was happening.

When I first met Mando on a hot August day in 1998 on the wide stone steps of Norlin Library at the University of Colorado, I was a premed student, enrolled in a collection of courses that had me culturing antibiotic-resistant bacteria and studying dissected cadavers. I was a girl with a goal.

It's plausible, then, that Mando's memory of what happened next is accurate. He claims that he saw me on campus a week after our initial meeting and greeted me with an enthusiastic, "Hey, Julie!"

I stared at him blankly and said, "Do I know you?" (I have no memory of this conversation, increasing the possibility of its veracity).

Overlapping social circles wound us past our lackluster meet-cute: we were young and dumb, but it turned out we were perfect for each other, Mando's evenness a complement to my excitability. We started dating a year later, and not long after that I abandoned the med school track as a result of the circulating horror stories about the course workload for organic chemistry and Mando's job prospects.

Though my prehealth classes didn't lead to a medical degree, they did have a lingering side effect: I have precisely enough medical knowledge to be a hazard to my own mental health.

Living in a world where so much can (and does) go wrong is a minefield for a perfectionist who prioritizes meeting expectations, who loves an equation that yields consistent results. I like to entertain the belief that if I make all the right moves, I'll win the game. But that's always been impossible. I know there are no moves to ensure, with total certainty, that I can have a life of happiness and protection, that I'll have a healthy, satisfying marriage, that my children will stay on the straight and narrow. I know there's no way to sidestep pain and loss, but it hasn't stopped me from trying.

In the days before Mando's return, I'd tried everything I could think of to pin down precisely what had gone haywire in my brain. I moved through my days in autopilot mode, experiencing the mild dissociation of the anxious: there, but not there. I felt wired and edgy, and my body sent unexpected panic signals at regular intervals throughout the day. But small, intervening moments of normalcy helped me convince myself that the situation was controllable. Denial is a girl's best friend.

That week I quit caffeine cold turkey, reasoning that it was making me jittery. I took naps in the afternoon, passed out on the couch in the fetal position while the boys sat at the coffee table doing their homework. If I didn't call The Night's event a panic attack, if I didn't say that something was wrong, if I just waited and drank less coffee and rested a bit more, then perhaps this would sort itself out.

I didn't have a clue as to what was really happening inside my brain. It wasn't until I read *The Body Keeps the Score* by Bessel A. van der Kolk, months later, that I understood. Our body has a "window of tolerance," in which the rational and emotional portions of our brains are balanced. The amygdala is the emotional part of our brain, the more primal of the two: its ordinary job is to be "a quiet background presence that takes care of the housekeeping of the body, ensuring that you eat, sleep, connect with intimate partners, protect your children, and defend against danger." But if, for example, a patient (me) is in a state of hyperarousal and exceeds that window of tolerance, the alarm system of the amygdala becomes overly sensitive, causing the person (me) to feel highly reactive, panicky, and disorganized.

I was in a state of intense hyperarousal, and my on-fire amygdala was Cruella de Vil behind the wheel, driving like a bat out of hell and making zero stops. The rational part of my brain, the part centered around the dorsolateral prefrontal cortex, was left in the dust.

The dorsolateral prefrontal cortex (rational) and amygdala (emotional) have no direct connections in our brains, but they're bridged by the medial prefrontal cortex, which is the brain's center of self-awareness. Self-awareness, in this case, refers to *interoception* (Latin for "looking inside"), which is an ability to observe our inner experience.

To calm my amygdala and stop hearing alarm bells from every corner, I needed to slow down and become self-aware. I needed to pay attention to my emotions, to feel what I was feeling in both my mind and my body, in spite of its awful discomfort.

But in my experience, motherhood creates major hurdles to attending to one's own needs. Slowing down, connecting to our inner lives, making space to examine our own emotions: these aren't behaviors that are easily balanced with parenting children, particularly young children. We begin early by denying our own need for sleep, responding instead to cries in the night. But the primal focus on the needs of others outlives its usefulness. It's the reason my friends and I will rush our children in to the urgent care to rule out an ear infection, but we ourselves will cough, hack, and bladder-leak our way through the entire month of February until finally going in to find we've developed walking pneumonia.

Mothers are many things to many people, often at the center of the wheels of their families' lives. And it's a gift to be needed, to be seen, to know that our lives are interconnected to the lives of our people. But if we love our lives and people and we listen to even a handful of the messages about what it means to be a good person or a good partner or a good parent, then we may begin to believe we can't stop turning, cannot possibly stop perpetuating the revolution of the lives at the periphery of our wheels. Slowing down ceases to register as an option. After all, I'm bound to these people by love and proximity and the thousands of tiny tasks that fill our days together. *I love, therefore I do* quickly warps into *I do, therefore I am.*

I filled Eli's water jug from the fridge, paying close attention to the level so as not to spill it all over the floor. I was looking at the water—not at Mando—when I said, without emotion, "I was just really scared that I was going to have another reaction and you were gone and there would be no one there for the kids if something happened to me."

My words diminished the experience: "Just scared." *That's all, Julie? You were just scared your life was coming to an end that very night?*

Mando stopped his movements to look at me, concerned but focused.

On paper, he should've been the more fearful of the two of us, having experienced more than his share of loss in his life. Mando's mom, Becky, had died tragically when he was sixteen. They had been driving as a family on I-25 South from Colorado Springs to Pueblo when a car shot across the wide grass median and crashed into their minivan, killing Becky and injuring both Mando and his sister, Gina, who was only thirteen at the time. The impact of the accident showed all over Gina's life—understandably so. But Mando was a little more like his mother—remarkably tough, exceedingly resilient—and his response to nearly any situation was to stick to the facts.

"The nurse told you what happened after the shot won't happen from being outside and getting regular allergy symptoms?" he asked.

I pulled the jug away from the fridge and nodded as I screwed on the lid, making sure it was secure. "Well, yes."

"Okay," Mando said, nodding as he grabbed energy bars from the pantry and dropped them into my oversized purse. *Okay* translated to *Well, glad that's settled.*

"The thing is, I still feel stressed out," I told him. Trying to describe the intensity of what I'd been experiencing since that night remained out of reach.

Eli emerged from his room at that moment, needing help with his belt. Nolan started telling me something that happened during a school assembly while Eli struggled to get on his damn cleats. My conversation with Mando was cut short by the chaos of leaving the house.

So we left it there. We abandoned this completely inadequate, unfinished discussion of my basest, most primal fears. We left those tender, exposed parts of my heart lying unprotected there on the counter next to Eli's water jug, which we forgot to put in the car.

7

A MONTH BEFORE THE NIGHT I Couldn't Turn Off the Lights, Mando and I sat opposite each other in window seats on a high-speed train from Brussels to Paris. It was a crisp, sunny morning, and we shot through the countryside, each of us gazing out the windows of the train at the verdant hills zipping past, their surfaces peppered with small cottages, farms, cows. We had traipsed through Amsterdam and Brussels over the previous four days, adults indulging in the thrill of ditching school, our caregiving responsibilities left to my mom, who was watching baseball games from the car at the sports park to avoid the wind chill that made fifty degrees feel like twenty.

Joie de vivre may be a commonly used phrase in English, but the French own the rights to the concept. Paris was magical. Less than twenty-four hours walking those streets convinced me I was meant to be French. All I needed was a scarf and a baguette, and *voilà*, I was Parisian. As an unexpected bonus, my two years of high school French came back to me, enabling simple, amiable exchanges with shopkeepers and taxi drivers. Mando was genuinely surprised that I spoke that much French, and there was a unique pleasure in impressing him, the man in my life who's not easily impressed.

I cried when I first spotted the Arc de Triomphe from the back of a taxi, a moment that will remain mine, a moment I was free to inhabit with all the attention it deserved. I didn't have to look away to dig in my purse for a banana because someone was hungry, wasn't tempted to attend to someone's questions or give a history lesson that zero people would retain or care about.

For those days in Europe, I was able to revel in the wholeness I so rarely glimpsed in my life. I was happy and present; Mando and I were present together.

But, true to form, I hadn't been sure leaving the kids was the right move.

Just before we left California, Mando and I were emerging from the tail end of a virus, one that had most likely borne into our midst on the backs of our carrier monkey children. The four of us had hacked, coughed, and sneezed our way through the last two weeks of March. I was exhausted by the time my mom arrived from Japan to care for the boys. She and I sat on the floor of my bedroom on the night before the trip, sorting through toiletries on the wool chevron rug. Because my mom knew my tendency to be—*ahem*—tightly wound, she listened when I told her I was nervous.

"I always feel unsure when I leave the boys," I told her. "I just feel . . . *off.*" The exact source of my discomfort lay somewhere at the intersection of my own perfectionist expectations of myself, mom guilt, and the pervasive social messaging about the sacrifices expected of a Good Mom. Leaving my children felt akin to a dereliction of duty, a questionable choice just short of going AWOL.

My mom tried to reason with me, her uptight eldest child, as she picked up a sample of night cream that grabbed her interest. "Julie, no one will care for your boys better than me," she said, reassuring me with the same words she'd used each of the few times I had left my children.

"I raised you and your brother and sister, and you all survived," she reminded me, putting down the night cream. She pawed through the rest of the items to see if there was anything she wanted to swipe.

"I know," I said. "But is it worth it to go?"

She stopped what she was doing and looked straight at me. "To see these places you've always seen on television and actually *be* there? To walk under the Eiffel Tower with Mando? Yes, it will be worth it. It's going to be wonderful."

It's going to be wonderful, I thought.

After putting the boys to bed, Mando and I dosed ourselves with supercharged, codeine-laced cough medicine, hoping that we could get a few hours of solid sleep before we left early the next morning. Emotions and thoughts pinged through me like a series of pinballs: ambivalence, "normal" travel anxiety, "abnormal" travel anxiety, anticipation, excitement, mom guilt, daughter guilt (because the poor woman didn't know what she was in for). But the cough medicine pushed me to the edge of sleep, that semiconscious state that arrives just before you either pass out or wonder if you remembered to lock the front door and have to drag yourself out of bed to double-check. But instead of thinking about the door, my mind launched another possibility in that in-between space: *What if I'm allergic to this cough medicine?*

The adrenaline jolted me awake. I decided to take Benadryl—just in case. I walked past the boys' bedrooms to the kitchen, stepping lightly in the dark house. I shook the pink tablets into my hand, swallowed them, and then tiptoed back to my room, sliding into bed next to Mando, counting my breaths until I fell asleep. The experience was a precursor, a warning shot from my body.

The next day, we boarded the flight to Amsterdam, and I cued up a movie on my iPad. *The Fault in Our Stars*, packed with themes of loss, was a terrible choice. My quiet tears throughout the film did nothing for my lingering congestion.

Mando and I landed in Amsterdam and tried to make the most of the day, walking around the city, the cold temperatures keeping us alert when the jet lag threatened to pull us under. We made it until 7:45 p.m., when Mando fell asleep sitting up in the hotel bar, glass of wine in hand. We both crashed hard, but I popped awake at 2:00 a.m. and passed two dark hours with a book on my Kindle. When Mando ripped open the curtains at 8:00 a.m. (he might as well have gone full middle-aged dad and said, "Don't want to sleep the day away!") I was so pissed off I didn't speak to him for thirty minutes. He texted my phone while I was in the shower to apologize.

But by the time I was speaking to him again, as we ate our pancakes at the restaurant next door, I could feel a gentle shift. The seeds of anxiety that had begun to sprout the night before the trip lay suddenly dormant, their growth arrested by an opportunity for self-care, for connection, for relaxation.

All I had to do was be present. I love bikes, and Amsterdam was full of them. There was a trio playing Vivaldi outside the Rijksmuseum. Mando had planned our trip to suit us: we walked, laughed, took a million photos, and enjoyed hotel sex (enjoyed sex—full stop—without having to worry about whether the bedroom door was locked, whether we were safe from the libido-killers watching a Marvel movie in the other room).

Amsterdam to Brussels, Brussels to Paris. By the time I spotted the Eiffel Tower, I had left behind the myriad roles that defined my days, that were beginning to define me. I was back in my body, back in myself.

The trip offered a reprieve from parenting, which, though a privilege, can be a stifling, consuming business. Parenting looks less like a touching phone company commercial and more like cohabitation with small, emotionally labile narcissists whose needs are innocent but insatiable. If parents aren't terribly careful or terribly lucky, the required attention and preoccupation can harden like sedimentary rock, crushing the adults—and their relationships—beneath their combined weight.

Afternoon baths in a gorgeous hotel room, Versailles, the *Winged Victory* at the Louvre, a day trip to Champagne—in between these moments, Mando and I caught glimpses of who we truly were: content people.

We departed from Charles de Gaulle on a cloudy morning. It's no wonder that while we waited in line on the jetway, Mando glanced back at me to find my eyes welling up.

"I had trouble leaving, and now I don't want to go home," I

said. I knew that the dormant seedlings of stress would sprout when watered with schedules and obligations. I preferred the idea of staying in Paris.

Mando cracked a smile, and I started to giggle at the irony, wiping away the tears.

8

WHEN I WAS IN ELEMENTARY school, we were sometimes asked to create a diagram showing the plot of a book we were reading in class. My diagrams all had a similar shape: a small, uniform staircase, plot points tidily listed on each step, a climax at the very top, and then a downward step marking a resolution. Easy to see, easy to complete. But when you're living inside the plot, it can be more challenging to discern when something important is happening. It's only in retrospect that you can write in the little label on the step.

Just days after we got home from Paris, I received an email from my exercise studio, The Bar Method. I'd been working out there for nearly two years at that point. Even as I'd added working nearly full-time hours in the library, I'd managed to get to the studio at least twice a week, hauling ass north on the freeway, often jogging into the class from the parking lot, skidding in the door as the instructor was beginning the warm-up or, if I was late, the first set of push-ups. But once I was through the door, I had one full hour of nothing to think about except the workout. Someone directed me, corrected my form, encouraged me. I had friends there, and after inviting my best friend, Allie, to a class, we tried to sync up our schedules and go together as often as possible.

The short email I received from the owners was as direct and to the point as the teachers were when they adjusted our positions in class: the studio was closing in two weeks.

Even my mom, who doesn't share my love of exercise, was a little flustered when I told her the news, her tinny voice echoing from the phone speaker on FaceTime as she said, "But Julie, you love going there!" Amy was bummed for me, and Mando knew I would miss that time.

I didn't complain outside my inner circle. Who was there to complain to? What difference would it make? It was blatantly—uncomfortably—a first-world problem. Would I also be complaining that my diamond slippers were too tight?

These things happen, of course, and it would've been unremarkable if life had been a bit more balanced, or if I'd found something to replace that time, those endorphins. But I didn't.

Six weeks before The Night I Couldn't Turn Off the Lights, I stopped exercising, and what should've been a footnote became a plot point, a step on the staircase of my increasing burnout.

9

THE TRICK ABOUT MENTAL HEALTH is that when you discover—or admit—you need support, all the tools you would
use to find that support have vanished. You're hopelessly tired,
easily confused, fatigued by even the slightest roadblock. What a
perfect time to navigate our breezy, welcoming medical system.

Nearly a week after The Night I Couldn't Turn Off the Lights,
Mando and I sat on the couch to watch a Conan O'Brien special.
I'd been trying to flip my internal switch back to the off position,
but it refused to budge. Though I'd dropped caffeine, I felt a constant buzz punctuated by random spikes of adrenaline. I took
naps, but I was less rested with each passing day, my overnight
sleep becoming an anxious, sweaty, nightmare-riddled affair. My
stomach churned, and so I ate next to nothing.

The more I failed to find traction, the more I panicked. Though
I recognized my anxious tendencies to like everything just so, this
was the first time I'd ever experienced capital-A Anxiety. It was
acute, and I was terrified.

I punched the buttons on the remote to start the program I'd recorded weeks earlier. The kids were in bed after a day of sports and errands: a textbook suburban Saturday. I sat in the far corner of the sofa, my legs tucked underneath me, my hoodie still zipped all the way to the top. The buzzing of my body left me constantly chilled.

Mando handed me a glass of red wine as he joined me. I thanked him automatically, my thoughts elsewhere. He knew I was not myself. And, more frightening, I knew I was not myself: I was quiet and edgy and emotional.

I was also out of energy. I took a deep breath and waited in vain for my body to calm, imagining this might be the moment when things would suddenly improve. I took a sip of my wine and set the glass back down on the coffee table in front of us. Mando picked up the remote and pressed play, giving me a gentle smile.

We made it through two segments. Mando laughed at the absurdity of Conan folding his impossibly tall body into a Fiat. He had just pressed play on the third segment when I interrupted. I sat up straight, put my hands on my knees, and said aloud, "I don't feel right." I started to cry.

I had been trying so hard, doing my type A level best to fix this, to extinguish the lights or, at the very least, lessen the blinding brightness of the Anxiety. Nothing had worked even a little—and I was exhausted. The lights stayed on, but they were stadium lights now, the wattage punishing.

I rubbed my hands on my jeans as I felt the panic rise, constricting my throat. I was shaky and sweaty, and my body was telling me to flee, but from what threat? I knew there was nothing to fear in that moment, but that did nothing to lessen my anxiety. If I couldn't see the enemy, couldn't name the problem, how could I combat it?

The lights burned and buzzed; I was bitter and deeply discouraged. Mando put his hand on my back as I perched on the edge of the couch, holding my head in my hands and feeling the angry, frustrated tears slip down my face.

I dialed my gynecologist's office first thing on Monday morning. It was perhaps a strange first step, but I liked Dr. Cooke: she was a woman, a mother, a no-nonsense communicator. She was also my friend Cathie's gynecologist and had recently referred her to an excellent specialist. Good doctors know good doctors, I reasoned, hoping she'd know an experienced therapist who could help me feel better.

"Hi," I said quickly, getting right to the point. "I'm a patient, and I'm looking for a referral for a therapist and wondering if you have any that Dr. Cooke recommends."

"Um, well, we don't really have that," the receptionist replied. She sounded as if she was doing something else. I could hear paper shuffling in the background among the common sounds of an office coming to life after the silent weekend.

"Well, can I make an appointment to talk to the doctor?"

"What would you need to see her for?"

I squeezed my lips together, feeling my brow crease. *Didn't I just say?* "I'm struggling right now with anxiety, and I need to get some recommendations."

"We don't really see people for that," she informed me. I was silent for a moment, stumped. I knew that it wasn't Dr. Cooke's specialty, of course, but since many women I know use their annual gynecological exam as a catchall, surely she had patients who experienced anxiety. I wasn't asking for an opinion on whether I should get bangs.

"Let me place you on hold," the receptionist said abruptly, sounding annoyed. She came back on the line with, "You should go see your primary care doctor."

"Right, but he's a man, and I want to talk to a woman I know, and I really think Dr. Cooke will have some guidance. Could you please give me an appointment?" I was doubling down. I needed this more than the receptionist needed to move on to her next task.

"Hold on." I could practically hear her sighing as she jabbed the button to silence our connection.

I waited, the phone in my hand. How had this conversation veered so sharply from what I'd anticipated? Why was I arguing with the receptionist and feeling like I was somehow inconveniencing the entire office by asking for care?

She came back and granted me an appointment for the following day.

Step one should've been easy.

I was attentively picking at my dry cuticles when Dr. Cooke opened the door to the exam room the next morning. The hardwood floors groaned as she stepped into the room and closed the door behind her. She wore scrubs that suited her athletic build, and her long, dark hair was pulled into a casual ponytail. She inspired confidence.

I was so hopeful she could help.

"What's going on?" she asked, perching on a stool next to the exam table.

I tried to find the right words—words that had previously evaded me in conversations with Mando, my parents, Amy, Allie, Cathie.

"Something has turned on and I can't turn it off and I'm a mess," I told her. I felt a slight release of pressure, delivering that sentence.

She looked at my face more closely. "Well. When did this start?"

I gave her a brief sketch of the preceding months, giving her the broad strokes of my life, work, and motherhood. I told her I'd had glimpses of this anxiety as it had advanced, mentioning the brief wave just before the trip to Europe that I'd been able to tamp down during our time away. Anxiety wasn't totally unfamiliar, I told her, but this felt different. This surge had tripped the circuit breaker. No matter what I did to try to calm down, my body stayed activated, my system pulsing and on edge. I didn't use the term *panic attack*. I cried as I spoke.

Dr. Cooke sat calmly, listening. I took a deep, shuddering breath and waited for her to respond.

"So you weren't feeling like this when you were on vacation?"

"No," I responded. I wasn't sure why that was important but trusted she was going somewhere with this line of reasoning. "I was a little anxious at the beginning, but that's normal for me when I'm traveling away from my boys."

"When you're not on vacation, when do you have time for yourself?" she asked, eyebrows raised.

I gave a sarcastic half-laugh, half-sob.

"Never," she said, answering her own question with finality. She pointed to a poster behind her, sloppily taped to the cabinets: Recess Is Not Optional. I stared at the poster.

Some self-saving part of me knew even then that I was far past just needing recess.

"I think I need some help figuring out how to turn off whatever has been switched on," I said, pulling the conversation back to my original intention. "I was wondering if you knew a good therapist. Or maybe my thyroid is off?" I nurtured a flickering flame of hope that this was a purely physical problem that could be fixed with the pop of a pill.

Dr. Cooke didn't seem to hear me. "Do you have a clone? If not, there's no way you can do all the things you just listed. Your job is too much."

I nodded, but only because I felt off-balance, in the same way I laugh awkwardly when I can't hear what someone's said to me and can't possibly ask them to repeat their statement for a third time.

I was so terribly raw. Could she see this? How could she *miss* it? I expected my confession would elicit compassion, solidarity, guidance; I expected her to tell me that I was okay, that there was a path forward. Instead, she finished weighing the evidence and presented her conclusion succinctly with a single shot of advice.

"You need to quit your job," she said.

I hesitated, frantically trying to organize my thoughts. We were no longer slightly off course; we had jumped tracks. Even the briefest look at my chart would have informed her that the Julie she saw last year was vastly different from this Julie—I'd lost significant weight, and I couldn't imagine that my blood pressure hadn't increased since I practically vibrated with anxiety. This Julie was a shell of that one. She thought my job was to blame for that? How could the calculation be that straightforward?

"And a therapist, yes. You got it." She handed me a slick purple referral card with a headshot of a happy-looking brunette. As I scanned the details, I heard Dr. Cooke talking again. "Dr. Fischer is my therapist and has weekly group Zoom calls." I nodded mutely. What the hell was a Zoom call?

"I'm also going to give you a prescription for Xanax." She pulled the prescription pad from the drawer, scrawling the dosage and directions in blue pen before expertly ripping off the sheet and handing it to me. I took it. Reflexively, I thanked her. She clapped her hands together, as if applauding herself for having solved my problems. She stood up from the stool. I slid off and picked up my purse from the chair next to the exam table.

When we reached the counter by the receptionist, she delivered the rest of her plan. "I'm going to write you a note," she said, definitive and conclusive. "It says that you're quitting, effective . . ." She trailed off, raising her eyebrows to indicate I should finish the sentence.

I stared at her blankly.

She prompted me, clearly waiting for me to respond with her predetermined correct answer: "Today or next week?"

"Today?" I hoped it was the password that would grant me a swift exit from this moment, this office, this train wreck of an appointment that I'd set in motion. I'd insisted on it, in fact.

"Good," she said. "That was a test. You're going to feel how I felt when I stopped delivering babies."

How would I know how she felt when she stopped delivering babies? Happy? Good? Relieved to not see tiny coneheads emerging from vulvas all day long? I didn't ask for clarification.

"Okay, thank you." I took the note from Dr. Cooke's outstretched hand and let the autopilot Me take over. Say thank you again. Say goodbye now. Open the door. Walk through it. Don't cry. Close the door. Down the stairs. Get into the car.

My car was a sauna. I rested my head lightly on the steering wheel, the leather sticky and hot against my forehead.

I, a grown adult thirty-eight-year-old woman, held a permission slip in my hand. Dr. Cooke had written me a prescription to quit my job, as if a major life decision required only a hastily jotted approval.

If I hadn't been so crushed, I would've laughed at the absurdity of it.

I should've laughed at the absurdity of it. Though the job brought chaos, it had also been a source of joy. I was appreciated and seen; even if it wasn't perfect, it was a logical and natural fit. Was the job really the problem? I didn't want to believe that.

But as a seed of doubt rooted itself in my fragile mind, I was suddenly unsure: *do I need to quit my job?*

I glanced at the clock on the dash; first-graders would be lined up on the rainbow rug in less than thirty minutes. I wiped my eyes, checked my mirrors, and backed out of the parking spot very carefully. *The last thing this morning needs is a fender bender*, I thought to myself.

I drove to school scrolling through a mental book catalog to choose a read-aloud while simultaneously wondering whether the job that was perfect for me, the one that had unexpectedly ushered me back into the working world after ten years, would have to go.

Advice—even shortsighted, hasty, questionable advice—isn't easily dismissed when you're desperate.

10

WHEN ELI WAS IN FIRST grade, his classmate Trevor punched him in the stomach at recess, out of sight of the teacher. Trevor had been a turd all year, and in the preceding months, Eli's reports of shoves and name-calling had slowly increased. I counseled him with all the typical approaches, but nothing was bringing resolution. I would occasionally daydream about giving little Trevor a piece of my mind and maybe slashing his bike tires but didn't indulge the thoughts for too long. Though tempting, intimidating first-graders didn't seem like the right approach.

After the punch, Eli seemed genuinely upset about the seemingly inescapable situation. Uncharacteristically, he said he didn't want to go to school the next day.

That evening, after tucking Eli in bed, I emailed his teacher, Ms. Green.

Her kind and quick response: "Hmm. It sounds as if we should have a phone call."

When we spoke the following evening, I gave Ms. Green the rundown, explaining that my main concern was Eli's growing stress.

"I'm not sure how I should direct him," I said.

"I think the best thing to do," Ms. Green said, "would be to help Eli regain his confidence in handling this difficult dynamic himself. So perhaps you could tell him something like, 'Eli, I *know* that you will know how to handle things with Trevor if something happens. You can tell him you don't like it, you can talk to Ms. Green, or you can walk away. But whatever happens, I'm confident that you'll know what to do.'"

I let out a relieved sigh. That, I could do.

And if it proved ineffective: the tires.

The next afternoon, I met Eli at the school gate so we could ride our bikes home together. As we maneuvered to escape the dismissal crowd, I registered Eli's smile, his relaxed shoulders. When we broke free, I put my foot up on the pedal as I waited for him to fasten his helmet. I took advantage of the lack of eye contact, saying, as casually as possible, "So how'd it go with Trevor?"

"Good," Eli reported. "He pushed me a little today, but I yelled, 'Stop it!'" He kicked off the ground and pedaled ahead of me to the wide paved path running through our neighborhood that would take us home. And just like that, the Trevor situation was behind us.

As it turned out, the bigger problem wasn't Trevor but Eli's crisis of confidence. Ms. Green's advice was both timely and timeless. Her careful words that evening permanently shaped aspects of my parenting. Thanks to her counsel, I ask the boys questions like, "Well, which way are you leaning?" or "What's your gut on this?" And even now, we conclude plenty of tangled conversations with, "You can trust that you'll know what to do when the time comes."

After my appointment with Dr. Cooke, this simple assurance—the one I so desperately needed—was inaccessible to me. My confidence had been badly shaken; I was deeply unsure of my ability to handle regular life, to say nothing of the endless frightening possibilities that played on a loop in my head.

If you can't trust your own inner voice, then what?

I walked down the hall to the principal's office, passing the happy noises emanating from the kindergarten classrooms, punctuated by exclamations and the gentle redirections of the teachers. A student banished to the hallway to finish an assignment saluted me with a chipper "Hello, Mrs. Chavez," in order to further procrastinate writing out the alphabet on the lined sheet of paper. "Oh, do we have library today? And can I get the book that Dominic had?" The kids had been clamoring over Robert Munsch's *Purple, Green, and Yellow* since I'd introduced it as a read-aloud. It had been one of Amy's all-time favorite books, and reading to the students about Brigid drawing on herself with super-indelible-never-come-off-till-you're-dead-and-maybe-even-later coloring markers was as much fun for me as it was for them. I loved watching their little expressions evolve from shocked to perplexed to intrigued by Brigid's naughtiness. I gave a little disclaimer about not drawing on ourselves after each reading, just in case.

"No library today for you, but you can check that one out as long as Dominic returns it," I said, answering without breaking stride, refusing to get sucked in by his delaying tactic.

I loved this job; I was perfect for this job; the job was too much. Perhaps all of these things were true. I didn't know anymore.

I don't know if I can do this job next year, Shay. I practiced saying it to myself as I walked through the main office to her door.

I knocked on the open door and stuck my head inside.

Shay was looking at her computer as she nodded and slowly said, "Yes . . . just give me a . . . second." She finished typing and made two quick, satisfied clicks with the mouse before looking up at me. "Done. What's up?"

Her expression slid from curious to concerned as she registered my uncharacteristic brittleness, drawn face, and puffy eyes. She stood up and, as I sat down in front of the desk, closed the door behind me. I started to cry as she returned to her seat and placed a box of tissues between us.

"Julie, are you okay?" Shay moved through most of her days like a sprinter, a tiny powerhouse of efficiency commanding the nearly eight hundred students in our elementary school, but now she sat still, waiting for me to respond. Her hair was shaped into a fashionable bob with gentle waves; her blue eyes, the sort that crinkled happily when she smiled, were wide and waiting, focused on me.

"Well, no," I said, with a short sob. "I'm sort of losing it. I don't know if I can do this job next year, Shay."

I had hoped to feel relief after releasing the words but was instead slammed by a wave of helplessness. I didn't want to quit this job, but I was *desperate* to feel better. I needed to feel better.

"What's happening?" she asked.

"I think I'm having a nervous breakdown. I don't know if maybe the job is too much. Mando is traveling all the time and the boys have so much happening and I'm totally overwhelmed." I grabbed a tissue and Shay slid the box a little closer to me, her brow furrowed. She waited for me to go on.

"I went to see my gynecologist hoping to get a recommendation for a therapist, and she told me I needed to quit my job." Shay's eyebrows lifted. "At first I thought she was wrong. I mean, I love what I do. But I'm just not sure."

She nodded. "Well, I can't answer for you, but I do know that this is something that can happen when you go back to work, Julie. The working-mom meltdown is a real thing. My husband once had to come home from a trip to England when the kids were little. I called him and told him to get on a plane that day, and he had to pay a ton of money to change his ticket."

I laughed through my tears. It felt impossibly wonderful to find something funny, to feel solidarity and comfort.

"Julie, this is a real thing," she repeated. "There are tricks you have to learn. Like when the kids have events, you always sign up to bring salad because you can buy it in the bag. Or bottled waters." I remembered I needed to bring snacks for both boys' baseball games later that week. I'd been chafing all season long at the stupidity of it. At the beginning of the season, I had gently suggested that snacks were superfluous, contending that they weren't four years old anymore and therefore didn't need rewards for managing to tie their own cleats and walk upright on two legs. But some of the other moms had disagreed. So I'd signed up. Why did I always sign up?

Shay tilted her head. "Again, I'm not you, but I did happen to notice that you're still volunteering in the classroom, even though you're now *employed* here."

I nodded, tears still sliding.

She softened her voice before she said, "I think talking to someone is a really good idea. You have your review with me next month, right?"

I nodded again.

"Okay, so let's talk about the job then. I think you need to take care of yourself for now. We don't need to decide anything today."

Nod, hiccup. We both stood and she walked around to the door, opening it with her right hand as she squeezed my shoulder with her left.

"Thank you, Shay."

I walked back to the library, reversing my path down the shiny floors of the hallway. The student had managed only to write letters *A* and *B*.

"Twenty-four to go, buddy. Get that pencil moving."

As I walked past him, the pasted-on teacher smile faded from my face as the anxiety began to spike again. I may have been moving, but I certainly wasn't making progress.

Since I couldn't puzzle out my next move, the logical step was to begin polling those closest to me. Though our tight budget was greedily gobbling up the extra income, we weren't solely dependent on my job. To even consider quitting was a privilege afforded to me that, even in crisis, many women don't have. As *should I or shouldn't I* became my rumination of choice, my desperation leaked into my relationships, creating unbalanced conversations that always centered on me. It seemed all I had to offer was my corrosive need.

I called Amy while I was home from school for lunch, the house quiet. She was at work but picked up, walking away from her desk to take yet another phone call from me. She listened as I cried and told her how scared I was. "Amy, do I quit the job? I just don't know what to do."

"Not yet, sissy. Don't do anything right now."

In the evening, my mom and dad FaceTimed me as they drove to Costco in Japan. "I'm not sure if I should quit," I told them.

My mom was careful but supportive when she responded with "Julie, if it's going to make you feel better then I think it's fine to let go of the job. I had a really hard time working when you guys were young because it created too many moving parts."

Dad nodded along with Mom's assessment but weighed in with "I don't know, Jules. I think it might be good to wait on this one."

Cathie came over the next night after the boys were tucked in bed. Mando was out of town, and I sat cross-legged next to her, turning my water cup around and around in my hands as we sat on the couch. She couldn't believe Dr. Cooke's advice, asking, more than once, "She said *what?*" She was especially emphatic that there was no urgency in making this decision, pointing out that I had manufactured a deadline in thinking that I had to decide now for the upcoming school year. "Julie, people quit midyear all the time, so if you start in the fall and it's too much, you can leave. I don't think you can know that right now. Just finish this school year. You're almost there."

But I was wired and stressed, my exhaustion growing by the day. Something had to change.

Out of all my people, Mando was trying hardest to figure out the situation—and me—looking, as he always did, for the shortest distance between the problem and the solution.

We stood together in the kitchen one evening as he made dinner for the boys. I perched on the barstool across from him.

"I don't think Dr. Cooke was right, but I do worry about the job overwhelming me because I'm doing way too much."

"What do you mean?"

"It's a lot—the job, the kids, school, baseball or whatever sport, volunteering, laundry, *all of it*. I feel like there's not a spare minute in my schedule." I reached in vain for the words to adequately describe my packed days. And what remained unspoken was the mental load: the intangible, invisible stresses that hide in between the items on the list. Even love and care—so necessary and beautiful in family life—have a cost.

"Well, nothing has slipped around here," he said.

"Right, but that's *insane*," I said. He looked surprised by the force of my tone, his eyebrows raising a fraction before he turned to pull shredded cheese out of the refrigerator. "I added thirty hours of work to my already busy week, and nothing in your life has changed? That's not normal." Bills, rides, coordination of the kids' schedules, dentist appointments and allergy shots and mail-in ballots, buying socks and underwear for growing children: I still managed it all.

"Okay," he said, clearly not sure where to step. "Look, I'm just telling you what I see."

"So do you think I should quit?"

"I don't know, Julie. I really don't think that's it."

"Allie thinks I seemed like I was more relaxed when I didn't have the job. And she's right." Strangely, I hadn't spoken to my best friend about any of what was happening until after my appointment with Dr. Cooke. But as soon as I began polling, Allie was promptly added to the list of regular consultants. Of course, she had noticed I wasn't quite myself: I sent fewer ridiculous GIFs, didn't regularly attend our book club, and often seemed distracted and preoccupied. But she didn't want to add additional stress by broaching the topic; even among friends, this is terribly normal. How do you tell someone you love that you miss them without seeming needy, that you're worried about them without hovering like an overprotective mother? The right words often escape us.

Mando used the tongs to check the underside of the quesadilla before setting them on the cutting board and turning to me.

"Okay, so then maybe you need to quit," he said matter-of-factly. "We can figure that out."

"But I think I won't have enough to do if I quit. Or, worse, what if I quit and I don't get any better? It's not like I can get this job back, and a school job is really my only option since the schedule matches the boys'. And we're definitely using that money."

A small muscle in his jaw flexed as he flipped over the quesadilla to brown the second side. "I don't know, then. We can figure it out if you need to quit, but again, I'm not sure that's the answer." I had talked us around and around in tiny, frustrating circles.

I thought someone could tell me what to do. But even when Dr. Cooke did just that, it wasn't enough. The person I needed to hear from was me, but my voice was conspicuously absent. I filled the silence with all these opinions, but the undertow of the polling succeeded only in pulling me farther from the shore of myself. And, too, I drifted farther from Mando, who waited on the beach, wondering where his wife had gone.

11

I HAD MY HEART BROKEN for the first time when I was a sophomore in high school.

I picked up the phone to my dedicated second line on a snowy Friday night. My parents had acquiesced after tiring of sharing phone hours with a chatty teenager, especially when the boyfriend had entered the picture. Two of my friends were hanging out at my house on a Friday night. We'd just finished our Domino's Pizza.

"Hey, we should talk," he said.

My eyes widened at those death-knell words, drawing the attention of my friends, who leaned over to listen. As I covered the receiver of the '90s see-through phone, one of them hissed frantically, "Make him meet you in person. Let him know how badly he's hurting you." Teenagers occasionally give terrible advice.

He picked me up and we drove to a parking lot so he could tell me he wanted to date someone else. I wasn't shocked—he'd been making slow, strategic, not-so-covert moves in her general direction—but I was devastated. We had dated for a year and a half; he was my first kiss and my first young love. The streetlight above us in the parking lot illuminated the fat snowflakes drifting to the ground as I sat in the passenger seat and cried, abandoning all pretense of dignity.

I was flattened. I spent the winter months pretending that my heart wasn't shattered every time I saw his car or his face or his new girlfriend.

A few months later, I stood behind my chair and zipped up my backpack, preparing to leave the French class taught by my beloved volleyball coach, Liz Kitzmann—the woman we all hero-worshipped and called Kitz. She, of course, knew about The Breakup, but we had never discussed it.

She called me over to her desk as the other students filed out of the room.

Kitz was everything I wanted to be when I grew up. She was smart and intuitive, beautiful inside and out. She was a woman with presence, comfortable in her own skin. I couldn't have articulated this then; I only knew I idolized her.

She leaned forward, placing her elbows on the desk. I stood before her, my hands hooked into my backpack straps.

"You don't seem like yourself. I think you should talk to someone."

I stared at the poster of French vocabulary words on the wall next to her desk, the butcher paper stretching from floor to ceiling: *alors, quoi, en fait, allez.* I stared at the filler words, the bright bubble letters blurring as I blinked back tears. I was stranded in the adolescent wasteland of high emotion and low self-awareness, lacking words and names and tools to manage the depth of my very real feelings. I'd tried to mute the painful emotions, but in the process I'd unwittingly muted my natural state: bright, outgoing, bossy, confident.

"I don't *feel* like myself," I managed to choke out. And there was relief in speaking those words aloud, to admit that I felt like a fragile, empty shell. For that moment, I could stop pretending.

She nodded and wrote out her own therapist's information on a Post-it Note as I admired her manicure. Her magenta nails clicked gently against the pen as I waited. Then she walked around her desk to where I stood, placing the small paper into my hand. She hugged me and then stepped back to hold me by the shoulders and look at me face to face. "You're going to talk to someone." It was a directive, a promise, a benediction.

From there, my mom took action. She arranged the appointments, filled out paperwork, and drove me to my visits. Therapy wasn't yet widely normalized in 1995, so she took extra steps to make sure I would have privacy around this process. She spoke to our primary care doctor, and I started on Zoloft, an antidepressant that would give me an assist as I started therapy.

Over the coming months, my mom would drive our red Jeep Cherokee to Sudi's office every week, dropping me off at the front of the building. And every week, Sudi helped me to feel like myself again. She helped me recognize the sound of my own voice. She told me I could stop saying that someone "made" me feel a certain way, reminding me that I had agency, control over my reactions and my choices. For a time, I felt embarrassed that a breakup had sent me so low, but Sudi pointed out the strengths of being an emotional person. My time with her demystified therapy and destigmatized the need for it. I had locks. Sudi had some of the keys, but as we progressed in treatment, it turned out I'd had some of them myself all along. I'd simply forgotten they were there in my hand.

I stopped the regular visits a few months later when I had regained my footing. I weaned off the Zoloft as we spaced out my appointments.

Twenty-three years later, I clung to the memories of this rescue, the plan masterminded and executed by these three powerful women: Kitz, my mom, and Sudi. But now I was the adult. I'd have to be in charge of my own rescue operation.

The appointment with Dr. Cooke was a setback. Now, on top of my anxiety, I carried a new doubt around with me: *Was she right? Did I need to quit my job?* This doubt was amplified by the drumbeat in my head of *I don't feel like myself, I don't feel like myself, why don't I feel like myself, will I be able to feel like myself again, will quitting my job make me feel like myself?*

But the remaining shreds of my intuition—and shreds they were—continued to insist that I find a therapist, and so I did some homework.

Dr. Cooke's therapist, it turned out, was a quick dead end, her high hourly rate ruling her out right away.

I'd sourced two recommendations from a friend of a friend, a therapist who had since moved to Florida. Both websites were standard fare, offering the expected generic information. I cross-checked by typing each therapist's name into the Google search bar in a new window. I didn't see any red flags, like disturbing newspaper articles or pending malpractice lawsuits (even in desperation, I remained fastidious and mildly paranoid). I returned to the first website and clicked on the contact page, which displayed a stock photo of the ocean to the left of the pricing: this therapist charged $150 per fifty-minute session. I switched to the other window; that therapist charged $165.

Mental health may be invaluable, but we also had a mortgage.

I needed a therapist who accepted my insurance (and I felt intense gratitude that we had the coverage). I pulled my Aetna card from my wallet and entered the necessary information to generate a list. Then I repeated the Google vetting process.

I also called the office of our primary care practice, hoping that perhaps I could catch a break and they'd have a name to recommend that happened to be on the list that now sat on my desk. Though caring, the receptionist didn't have a ready answer. We both stalled awkwardly before she said, "I hope you find someone," and I ended the call.

I hung up frustrated by these failed efforts to find the help I needed: *people get therapy, so why is this so hard?* In between homework and questions and figuring out what the kids would eat for dinner, I managed to make four calls. I left four voicemails.

A few days later, I received a call from Kim, one of the therapists on my short list.

She listened to what was going on, and then—after one doctor's visit, hours of internet research, and ten phone calls—Kim said the magic words I needed to hear: "Would you like to come in this week?"

After we worked through scheduling, Kim took time to explain the parking situation at her downtown office. She tried to alleviate the small, controllable anxieties of the visit, to preanswer questions and eliminate some of the unknown. It was thoughtful and intentional, and these kindnesses were calming to my frayed, tired nerves.

Finally, I could make out the faintest outline of hope on the horizon.

12

I WAS TEN MINUTES EARLY—FIFTEEN, if you counted the time spent in the parked car. I arrived at Kim's building earlier than I would have previously considered reasonable. But I was desperate for relief from my buzzing, electrified mind and body. Because I hoped so fervently that she was the right next step, I couldn't wait to get started.

Kim's waiting room was small, square, and empty. I closed the door quietly behind me, walking a few steps to pick up the clipboard she'd asked me to fill out as a first-time patient. It was on the bench, precisely where she'd told me I would find it. A squat lamp softened the ubiquitous office-building fluorescent lighting. The sounds of trickling water flowed from the tinny speaker of a white-noise machine sitting beneath the bench.

I sat down in the chair, a task managed by the autopilot. A photo of Paris hung on the wall across from me: a blue bicycle leaning jauntily against the stone wall of a café. I had been so happy in Paris less than two months earlier. I prayed Kim could help me find my way back to the contentment and joy I found there.

After filling out the form, I grabbed my phone and sent a quick message to Amy, telling her I'd arrived at the therapist's office. Hoping to calm myself as I trembled, I tried to remember my experience with Sudi. I wished I'd kept a journal from that time, a written record of all the tools and wisdom that Sudi had shared with me. Setting aside the self-recrimination about my poor recordkeeping, I reassured myself: I knew therapy worked because it had worked for me in the past.

My phone beeped as my sister's text popped up on the screen: You've got this. Love you.

At four o'clock, Kim opened the door to her office. "Hi, Julie," she said. She gestured to the room behind her. I went in, hoping she could help me find a way out.

The office was painted a slightly darker shade than the waiting room, its shape another small square. I sank down onto a cushy brown couch across from Kim. She sat in her rolling office chair, her back to her narrow desk, only an appointment book and a laptop atop its surface. To my right was a bright window that occupied more than half the wall. The window looked directly out at the branches of a dogwood tree, each limb abundant with bright spring-green leaves.

Kim had the kind of smooth blond hair that fell in a long, face-framing bob, the sort of hair that I imagine always does as it's told. Her makeup was minimal and tasteful, and she wore a pale pink blouse and a knee-length skirt. She was professional, composed: a collection of clean lines, preparation, and excellent posture. I was the opposite. I was edgy, inside and out, a fragile collection of barely attached pieces. My inability to eat was persisting, and my jeans hung off my frame. My hoodie was zipped all the way up.

Kim smiled as she crossed her ankles and arranged her skirt. "I'm glad it worked for you to come today," she said. From there, she took us through a series of inquiries intended to make sure that our circles didn't intersect. The social connections of parents with school-age children resemble vast spiderwebs of sideline acquaintances and familiar faces from PTA meetings. Once I approached a man at our local trampoline park and said, as kindly as possible, "I'm so sorry, but I'm just *sure* I know you from somewhere."

"You do," he said amiably. "I'm your dentist."

Kim's two girls were older than my boys, finishing out their high school days, and even when they were young, they'd attended an elementary school across town. I was relieved that our lives seemed to be on parallel tracks even within the same larger community. Another hurdle cleared. Relative anonymity is part of the safety of therapy, a necessary freedom to encourage openness. It felt like an auspicious beginning for Kim and me.

She looked down at the form I'd completed in the waiting room. "So, you work at a library? How is that?"

"Well, it's good. It's at my kids' school and . . ." I trailed off. "Is it okay if I just talk?" The sooner I began, I reasoned, the sooner I'd have this solved, and the sooner I could feel like myself again.

"Of course," she said.

For the next thirty-five minutes, I cried and talked and talked and cried, mostly giving Kim a summary of the previous few months. I finished by blowing my nose, adding the tissue to the other seventeen in my lap that I'd intermittently pulled from the box on the side table.

"I don't know what's wrong with me," I said. "I feel like I'm having some sort of midlife crisis," I told her.

She paused, nodding. "I think you're a little young for that," she responded, "but I think you could be having a midmom crisis. You're at a point where the boys are starting to need you in different ways, and combined with you going back to work, it sounds like you're at a turning point that feels uncomfortable."

I considered this, wondering how much of what was happening to me was related to being in this middle place of life, of motherhood. My greatest fear when I thought I would die from anaphylaxis was what would happen to my boys—both in the short term and the long term.

Nolan and Eli changed my life in all the ways babies change the lives of their parents. But more than that, they changed *me*. They wrecked my world in the most beautiful way, upending everything with their joy and their wonder and their perfect little toes. The privilege of loving them humbled me. As they grew, the love wore away some of the more callused spots of my heart: my pride, my selfishness, my insistence on being right. Though I continue to exhibit all these tendencies, their love has been a gentle sandpaper, helping me become who I suspected I was always meant to be.

As I sat across from Kim on her brown couch with my sensitive, new-skinned heart, I admitted to myself that I could see an ending of this season of motherhood approaching fast: graduations, milestones, distance. These people who had changed my life would, in not too many years, leave to live their own lives—an experience that my own mom described as being fired from the best job she'd ever had.

After building a decade of my life around these loves, the mid-mom crisis arrived with questions. How could I let them go if I knew that I had no control, if I knew that the world was marked by precarity? And even if I could manage to let go: who would I be without them?

"Would you like to make an appointment for next week?"

I nodded in response to Kim's question, though what I wanted to do was stay parked right there on the brown couch until life was proceeding as normal, until—more specifically—I was proceeding as normal.

We set my appointment and I typed it into my phone. As we reached the door, I stopped. "So, until then, what should I do?"

Give me homework, I telegraphed. *Tell me what the next step is, and I'll do it. Anything to help me move forward.* I wanted to feel better. At the very least I wanted to feel less awful, to stop feeling so intensely anxious and vulnerable. I wanted Kim to give me a magic exercise to help me feel like myself again. Of course, I knew that wasn't how therapy worked. And yet I clung to the mirage of a quick fix, an instant reset, a circuit breaker thrown into the right position to stop my body from constantly pumping electricity through my system, fueling those bright stadium lights of anxiety.

"I think it's a good idea to take care of yourself and find space where you can," Kim said.

I thanked her quietly and left, walking down the hallway, past the CPR classroom and down the stairs into the small, tiled vestibule with a wall of mailboxes. I pushed open the door, passing from the air-conditioned climate into the early evening.

My limbs were heavy as I got in the car. The noise of the radio was too much for my raw system, and I reached to silence it. I liked Kim and she seemed kind, but I was too exhausted to evaluate our appointment. As I drove home, all I could discern was that the pressure release hadn't helped in the way I'd hoped it would. I still buzzed with anxiety. Kim and I were going to have to get to know each other.

This would take time.

13

I PULLED INTO THE DRIVEWAY after the less than ten-minute drive from Kim's office. Mando was washing dishes at the kitchen sink after feeding the boys an early dinner. He dried his hands as I put down my keys and purse.

"How'd it go?"

After my appointment finished, I felt as if I couldn't manage a full, deep breath. I assumed it was an aftereffect of the crying, akin to a toddler's posttantrum hitching breath. I took one of these jagged breaths before answering. "It went fine. I think it'll be good. I'm going back next week."

"Okay," he responded, waiting for more. We'd both been counting the moments until the appointment, anticipating it would be a hopeful turn. But Mando's hope was contingent on mine, so he waited in vain for what I couldn't give: assurances that I would soon be back to some semblance of the person he knew.

I shrugged. I saw his efforts to remain patient, to pose a productive question that wouldn't be discouraging for both of us, but he didn't have the vocabulary to inquire about what I was experiencing, just as I didn't have the words to describe it. We were lost in translation. So instead of saying I felt separated from everything around me as if a thin glass wall surrounded me on all sides, instead of saying that the glass muffled the sound and love and warmth I needed from my life, instead of saying that a solution for this felt so far away that it was nearly invisible to me, I said, "Yeah. She seems good."

And he said, "I'm glad you went to see her."

14

WE PURCHASED THE KING-SIZE BED when a job transfer brought us from Seattle to Northern California in 2014. Married just after college graduation, I wanted nothing more than a happy first year together for Mando and me. Naturally, I took a perfectionist's approach to relationships, studying best practices as though I'd be grilled on them in a final exam: don't go to bed angry; don't have a television in the bedroom; force him to read *The Five Love Languages* and talk about it ceaselessly. *Check, check, check.* My heart was in the right place. I believed that following these guidelines would insulate us against the bitter, freezing winds of distance. Distance was the great enemy, and I took that literally when we picked out a queen-size first marital bed.

Twelve years later, we left behind that bed when we moved to Pleasanton. The move hadn't been without its fair share of bumps because, as it turned out, 2014 was a terrible time to buy in our new town. After six rejected offers on homes I'd moved into in my mind, we were finally in escrow on a small, overpriced single-story house with a neglected lawn, a rusty swing set, and a willow tree outside the bedroom. Now we needed a new bed, and so we found ourselves wandering through the big-box mattress store on a July afternoon, sweaty and weary.

As Mando tested one of the beds for firmness, I tapped on my phone, my fingers sending yet another detail to our mortgage broker. I waited for the confirming *swoosh* before tucking the phone into my purse. I looked out the floor-to-ceiling windows of the cavernous retail space, gazing at the freeway and the cars zipping by, the blistering sun reflecting off their windshields. I hoped—desperately—that we were making the right choices, on everything from the move to the house to the bed. Mando rolled over to his side, bouncing slightly on the tight surface of the bare mattress.

Since those early newlywed days I'd discarded heaps of useless advice and ideas, and I'd also learned the difference between distance and space. Distance grew from the accumulation of tiny resentments, the swallowed frustrations that are an inevitable part of coexistence between two imperfect humans. Space, on the other hand, was a necessity, creating room for our deepest needs: respite, rest, recovery.

That first smaller bed hadn't provided the magical insulation from distance I'd imagined. We still argued, still harbored hurts and slights, and none of it was resolved by a queen bed. The smaller dimensions only lowered our quality of sleep. One of us often woke up and resettled in the guest bedroom, a wanderer in search of rest. Newlywed Julie might have been aghast at the thought of two beds, but she didn't have two young kids. She was *rested*. Thankfully, our marriage hadn't crumbled from occasional nights of sleeping apart. Two beds hadn't torpedoed our sex life or diminished our closeness, hadn't changed that Mando was the person I most wanted to see across a room. Two beds, in those early years, simply meant more sleep (and paradoxically, less arguing, because it turned out neither of us was at our best when we were tired).

I scanned the mattress outlet to locate the boys—five and seven at the time. They bounced happily on a mattress in the corner, and I carefully ignored an employee's bothered face. I was exhausted and sad: we had uprooted these happy, bouncy boys from the only home they'd known, from friends and schools and Central Market, a grocery store with child-size carts they pushed past the lobster tanks in their coordinating L.L.Bean rain jackets.

Nolan had been particularly frustrated a few days before the arrival of the moving truck, ranting about the school lunch schedule and how he didn't want to miss Thursday, the day of the week devoted to corn dogs on the menu.

"Pal, I know this is hard," I said. "What can I do to help you?"

He scrunched up his first-grade face and yelled, "You could let me stay until the end of the year so I can have a *corn dog!*" But of course it wasn't about the corn dog. It was about none of us being quite ready for this ending, this beginning, this *change.*

And it didn't help matters that we began our California life in a bland corporate apartment, our only acquaintance the faceless, angry downstairs neighbor who banged on his ceiling throughout the day, incensed to have children living above him. Our early local haunts were the LEGO store and the Meadowlark Dairy, where we went for the orange-vanilla swirl soft-serve ice cream that tasted just like a Creamsicle. We spent eight lonely weeks in our new hometown until we finally began swim lessons and I met Cathie, who would become my first California friend. I met Allie two weeks later; the boys started school; I found a yoga studio and rode my bike there after dropping Eli off for afternoon kindergarten. I remembered the advice my mom had shared during the many moves of my childhood: bloom where you're planted. I dropped seeds everywhere I could and hoped they'd find root. And, miraculously, they did.

I wanted to believe that Kim could help me plant new seeds, that I could bloom again. But growth is slow, and patience is hard when you're in pain.

That night in bed, still shaky from my first session with Kim, Mando and I lay back-to-back in the center of our luxuriously wide king bed, zipped together from shoulders to tailbone. The comfort of sex had eluded me since our return from Europe. I craved that connection but knew it required a vulnerability I couldn't possibly muster. Instead, I absorbed his warmth, his presence, his solid body there next to mine. I pushed my back a little into his. His proximity grounded me in the physical world, reminding me I wasn't alone.

We bought the bed for the extra space, but that night we met in our shared center. Our bodies communicated what words could not. Kim told me to find space for myself, but at that moment, I needed *this* space, tucked up against Mando, pushing the emptiness out to the sides of the bed. We fell asleep that way because we love each other and because, on that night, it was the best we could do.

15

F HOPE IS A DRUG, its hangover is despair.

I undressed in the darkened room while my massage therapist, Michelle, waited outside the door. Her small stereo played the sounds of a gentle thunderstorm as I folded up my clothes and placed them on the chair next to the table. I drew the covers up around my shoulders and settled my face into the cradle. My chest was constricted and tight, my shoulders knotted, my neck gripped in a vise. I was white-knuckled with tension and anxiety.

Michelle knocked softly, asking if I was ready before entering the room and closing the door quietly behind her. As she prompted me to settle in, I begged my lungs to take in a round, full, complete breath. They refused.

My body hummed at high frequency, and my brain scrambled frantically to assign reasons for my fear. I had hoped—so intensely—that seeing Kim would bring relief, that talking to her would, at the very least, begin to reverse my downward trajectory.

But my state of high anxiety had only intensified in the past two days. The shallow, hitched breathing that I'd experienced after the first appointment with Kim had persisted. Now I had a new worry: what if I was at the edge of a more intense mental breakdown? What if this didn't get better, but worse? Would I need to be hospitalized?

I knew this outcome would be unlikely, but my rational brain was no match for the tidal wave of anxiety.

"Relax," Michelle whispered. "Take a deep breath."

I couldn't follow those simple instructions. The next sixty minutes of the massage were intolerable. My body was rigid and inflexible, my muscles strung taut like guitar wires on the verge of snapping. Michelle continued to move gently about my body as tears leaked from my eyes.

HOPE: a massage would help my body relax.

DESPAIR: stillness seems to make everything worse.

The escape-room outing had been planned for weeks. I was exhausted and wired, but as I dried my hair and put on makeup, I mustered my inner Pollyanna, ordering myself to look on the proverbial bright side: *I'll be able to stay close to Mando, we'll have time with friends, and the boys will be fed, watered, and put to bed by someone who isn't me.* I finished coating my lips with gloss and then looked at myself in the mirror. *Come on, Julie.*

Mando and I were the first to arrive. The receptionist requested we place our belongings in one of the short, square lockers. As I set down my phone and purse, I felt the drop in my stomach, the hollowness in my legs. I closed the small door and turned the key, worries flooding in. *How big is the room? Will I feel claustrophobic?*

What if I lose it and have a panic attack in front of all of our friends? I found Mando and stood close to him as our friends arrived. Autopilot Julie managed the greetings and the hugs and the catch-up chatter so I could privately nurse my small concerns and huge fears. Cathie wasn't there, and my battle was still invisible to this group of friends.

Our twentysomething host appeared and the nine of us walked together down the narrow hall into the escape room. He allowed us to shuffle past him and then walked in behind us, blocking the light from the hallway. My heart pounded.

"Okay, everyone, this is where you'll be working on your mission to rob (*dramatic pause*) this (*dramatic pause*) bank. You'll notice"—he paused as he grabbed the door handle in his hand— "this door is not locked. It won't be locked at any time. You are free to come out into the hall and waiting room if you need." I swallowed, and my panic diminished to a simmer as I thanked God for small favors.

And though the next hour kept the symptoms on low heat as we solved puzzles and worked to "steal" a plastic gem the size of my fist, the anxiety flamed back as I clicked my seat belt in the car to head home with Mando.

And as he looked over at me, as he registered my distress and my quick blinks and my slide back into sadness, he stiffened his neck, and I understood that he, too, had been hopeful.

HOPE: a Friday night with friends would help me relax.

DESPAIR: distractions from anxiety are only temporary.

I took a bath in the morning on Mother's Day. I leaned back against the cool enamel as the bubbles accumulated in fluffy piles over my legs, a mountain range of small, rounded, French lavender–scented peaks. The boys had proudly presented me with a stainless-steel container of fancy bath gel from L'Occitane earlier that morning. Nolan watched as I read his card, wanting, as always, to make sure he'd hit the mark. It included a picture of me, a smiling stick figure with straw hair and a book in my hand. When I thanked him, he hugged me hard and said, "You're the best mommy." Then it was Eli's turn to wait as I took in his earnest declarations of love, the sweet words scrawled on a folded piece of paper. When I looked up at him he was proud and happy, satisfied with his effort. I spread my arms to embrace him, and as we separated, I said, "Thanks, guys." I looked at each of them in turn and reiterated what I often told them: "Being your mom really is my favorite job."

They smiled and I hugged them again, trying futilely to absorb their affection, to allow their love to soothe my worn nerves through osmosis.

I picked up a handful of bubbles to balance on my knee as Mando opened the door to the bathroom and handed me a mimosa. He paused to sit for a moment on the side of our clawfoot tub.

"I thought you would like a quiet Mother's Day," he said. I heard what he left unsaid: *I know you can't handle much more than this right now.*

He was worried about whether I was eating enough because it was becoming clear I wasn't. When we sat down to dinner the previous night, my stomach had churned with anxiety. Mando sat across from me as I pushed the food around on my plate—*back, forth, back, forth.* I forced down a few small bites to placate him, but he still looked concerned when he saw the amount remaining. As we did dishes together he said quietly, out of earshot of the kids, "You've got to eat, Julie." I nodded. I knew he was right, but my nervous stomach seemed only to want to be empty. I added it to the list of issues for which I didn't have a fix.

I watched the bubbles pile up and reached to adjust the water temperature, wanting it to be as close to scorching as possible. I looked back up at Mando to say, "Thank you. This is perfect. I wouldn't have wanted to do anything more than be with you guys." We briefly discussed a plan to watch a movie in the afternoon, and he left to manage the boys, closing the bathroom door quietly behind him.

I waited until I was alone to cry. I had woken early in a pool of sweat after a night of anxious dreams. The spiral was tightening, and I felt an additional layer of worry about my boys and how my anxiety might be affecting them. Though I was doing my best to shield them, careful to show appreciation for their kind gestures and utterances of love, I knew that children have a way of sensing what their parents try to hide.

I sat in the bathtub as the bubbles disappeared and the water cooled, my arms still wrapped around my knees. I only got out when my fingertips had morphed into flesh-colored raisins. I stood, grabbed my towel, pulled the plug, and prayed that some of my distress would run down the drain with the bathwater.

HOPE: I could find solace in the love of my family.

DESPAIR: I could no longer hide my pain from them.

16

I WOKE UP EARLY THE morning after Mother's Day, sweaty and shaky, fists clenched. I couldn't wait until Wednesday to see Kim—I was sinking too quickly. I needed to find a new source of hope.

Tim, the physician assistant we saw at our primary care office, had assisted us with garden-variety medical needs over the previous two years. After letting my school know I'd be in late and booking Tim's first appointment of the day, I sat in the waiting room trying to appear normal.

Maybe I fooled the woman sitting across from me. Maybe it seemed as if I were mindlessly scrolling through my phone. Maybe the anxiety that traveled up and down my body was invisible to her even as it consumed me: shaky thighs, roiling stomach, tight chest, whirling thoughts. The woman was round and curvy, whereas I had become edges and bony prominences and sharp angles, the result of an all-adrenaline diet. For the first and only time in my life, I thought to myself, *I want my love handles back.*

I don't want to disappear. Help me out of this, and I will never again think twice about my weight.

I may have been fooling her, but I was painfully aware of the depth of my misery. As I sat there, offering up these useless bargains, the door to the waiting room opened and the nurse called my name.

Tim walked into the exam room with a concerned smile, having read in the check-in notes that I was seeing him about anxiety.

He wore his standard uniform of wrinkle-free khaki pants, checked button-down shirt, brown shoes that were polished but not shiny. Tim was the boy next door. He was polite and kind, he listened and followed up (and follow-up from a caring medical professional: swoon). He rolled his mobile desk into the room, and I was crying before he finished closing the door. He handed me a tissue.

He waited for a beat, looking at me sympathetically. "What's happening, Julie?"

I began with our Europe trip and then walked him through the previous weeks, concluding with the description I'd landed on as closest to accurate. "It's like a switch has been flipped and now my body is always on. I can't get off the ride," I told him.

He had been listening attentively and paused, absorbing the last of my report. Then he looked at me and said, very gently, "Julie, you're definitely describing anxiety symptoms, but I actually think you might be depressed." Tim knew what the best medical professionals know: the presenting problem is rarely the root problem.

His words brought a tiny, unexpected wave of relief—as if my own inner voice distantly echoed its assent. I listened as Tim continued.

"Julie, I know you. You're a pretty resilient person. You're positive. You're an optimist. You usually understand how to get yourself out of a funk. You haven't been able to figure this out and bounce back, and I think that's probably what's making you anxious, since you're not used to it. And then feeling anxious makes you more depressed. It's a cycle that makes you more and more uncertain."

He waited for me to respond. I nodded slowly as I said, "I think you're right." I gripped the edges of the exam table as he continued.

"You have a lot happening right now. If you think about wellness like a wheel, there are all the spokes coming off the center: nutrition, stress management, exercise, sleep." He made the shape of the spokes in the air as he named them. "If you break one or even a couple, you can still keep moving, but if you snap too many, the wheel stops turning and collapses."

After weeks of disconnection and desperation, being heard and understood was a physical sensation, as if he was placing a warm, weighted blanket on my shoulders to ground me. I didn't realize how much I had faulted myself for my inability to get out of this slump. His words meant that I wasn't alone, wasn't wrong, wasn't imagining my misery or somehow causing it by making the wrong choices. I was depressed. Paradoxically, this felt like great news.

"I think we should start you on an antidepressant. I typically recommend Zoloft."

"I took that when I was in high school," I said. Why had I not thought of that before?

"Did it work for you then?"

"Yeah, it did. And I don't remember any side effects."

"Okay, great. We'll start you on a low dose," he began, then paused briefly as he typed the prescription into the laptop on his rolling desk and tapped at the screen with his stylus. When he finished entering the details, he looked at me again. "When you feel like you're drowning, you're too far under to use any of your skills. Nothing is working because you can't get your head above water to take a breath. The medication will throw you a life preserver. It will give you a boost to lift you up a little bit and give you a break so that you can start swimming."

"I hope this works," I said. And then I was crying, but in relief. The tunnel was still dark, but I could imagine a pinprick of light at the far end. What Tim said made sense. He finished entering information and looked up at me.

"I'm recommending this, but the most important thing is that you figure out how you got here, and that's where therapy will come in. I'm glad you're already talking to someone. You need to understand what happened so if this happens again, you'll know what to do sooner." Tim went on to prescribe Klonopin to cut down my anxiety in the near term, since Zoloft can take some time to start having an effect.

"Do you really think I need the Klonopin if I'm taking Zoloft?" I asked. Perfectionists don't like to need, to depend. "I'm not sure I want to take it."

"Julie, no one should *want* to take it, but this is what it's there for."

Tim ordered blood work to rule out other possible factors but told me he was pretty confident about this diagnosis. We said our goodbyes, made a follow-up appointment for a few weeks out, and I walked out into the bright sun to drive to the pharmacy.

Why hadn't I started with Tim? The answer was stupidly simple: I thought a woman would understand me better. I had powerful memories of the women who had rescued me over the years. But I failed to account for a key variable in my equation: each of those women really *knew* me.

There's no perfect approach to finding support. Communication in the midst of crisis is messy. Words fail us, and we're easily discouraged and confused. After weeks of false starts and wrong turns, I rediscovered pieces of hope because, as it turned out, Tim knew me too.

I called Mando as I drove to the pharmacy to collect my prescriptions. I merged onto the freeway when he answered after one ring.

"How'd it go?"

He said it in such a caring way that I nearly began to cry again. I wasn't the only one who felt vulnerable and exposed. "Good," I said, and I heard him exhale a bit. "Tim thinks I'm depressed."

"Okay, so what did he say?"

I parroted what Tim had explained to me. "That makes sense, Julie." He was grateful. Mando hated a lack of direction. And really, he hated to see me in pain, struggling against a problem that he couldn't solve.

"He gave me a prescription for an antidepressant, and I'm on my way to get it now. He said therapy was the most important piece, so it's good I'm already seeing Kim. The Zoloft typically hits full strength around a month."

"I'm so glad you went to see him," he said. "I have to go take a call, but I'll check in with you after. Drive safely and I love you."

"Love you too."

And though we had said those words countless times to each other in the years of our marriage, on that day, they meant more. That day they meant *your pain is my pain* and *I want a solution as much as you do* and, perhaps most important, *you are not alone.*

My brain was intent on making things difficult. After getting home from the pharmacy, I set the small paper bag containing the prescriptions down on the counter to wash my hands.

I removed a glass from the cabinet, filled it with water, and prepared to take my first dose of Zoloft. I took a few bites of a Clif Bar, and while I was chewing, because anxiety is a persistent bitch, I had a thought: *What if I'm allergic to this medication?*

The illogical thought parade picked up the pace. *What if this causes anaphylaxis? What if it doesn't work? What if it makes me feel worse? It could happen.*

My phone trilled—it was Amy. I picked it up to tell my sister I was afraid to take the meds.

"Julie, I love you. This is the right choice. Take the pill."

I asked her to stay on the line, feeling safer that way, as though she were next to me in the room. Before I could think any more, I popped the oblong, light-blue pill into my mouth and took a gulp of water.

"Okay, I did it." I began to cry.

"Julie, you won't be stuck here forever," Amy told me. "And I know it because I've *been* there. You've seen it. You will get through this." Her tone was firm, definitive.

"Okay, maybe I should take one of the Klonopin and try to take a nap." I was exhausted. The hope of the morning had dissipated like fog, dispelled by the unforgiving sun of my anxiety.

"You should *100 percent* take a Klonopin, Julie. Do it now and lie down."

I opened the bottle, placed the pill in my mouth, and hastily swallowed it down with the rest of the water.

"Okay," I told Amy, "I did it."

"Good. Now go lie down. I'll call you after work."

I grabbed a blanket out of our hall linen closet and lay down on top of my covers, tucking myself into the blanket as tightly as possible.

Mercifully, my swirling mind was no match for the powerful sedative effect of the Klonopin. I was asleep within minutes.

17

I CALLED MY SISTER EVERY single day in the month of May. We covered only two topics. The first was our dad's health.

In early May, my dad had come home from work and had opted to add in an extra workout by taking the stairs up to their twenty-third-floor apartment in central Tokyo. He came through the door pale and clammy with a soaring heart rate that refused to slow down.

My mom knew my dad's ability to push through pain, and she was concerned he'd already waited too long for a checkup. And because my mom is a quiet, sometimes diabolical genius, she solved the problem in her own way: She tricked him into going to see the doctor. She asked him for a ride to an appointment with Dr. Robinson, when actually, the appointment in question belonged to him. As part of the physical, the doctor performed an ultrasound to inspect my dad's carotid arteries. Based on those results (which were solidly less than ideal), Dr. Robinson ordered a CT scan, but the scheduling proved to be a challenge, leaving our family in a waiting game. Medical systems are a breeze to navigate in other countries too, it seems.

The second topic we discussed—over and over—was me.

"Amy, tell me I'm going to get better."

"You *will*, Julie. You're doing the right things."

I borrowed my sister's hope as I lingered in the liminal space, waiting to feel more like myself. Recovery is brutally slow when you begin, a road trip that commences on an empty tank. You have to push the car the first five miles before you even get to the gas station.

18

I'M SCARED I WON'T BE able to get out of this," I confessed to Kim in my next session. And then, in a much quieter voice: "Like, I'm worried I'll have to be hospitalized or something."

I'd white-knuckled my way through the days leading up to my second hour of therapy. I took the Zoloft every morning with a desperate prayer. Though I wasn't as fixated on dying from anaphylaxis, my fear had expanded, pumped full of the helium that fueled my anxiety. I saw danger everywhere, and nowhere more closely than within my own mind. What if I couldn't recover from this? What if I never felt like myself again? How long could I tolerate this existence—not eating, barely sleeping, going through the motions of the day, constantly on edge? I was terrified of leaving my family, of sliding away from Mando and the boys.

Kim leaned forward as she rearranged her crossed legs. "Julie, I think that a lot of your fears are based in what *could* happen. You're trying to control those future events."

"You mean how I'm worried that if I don't maintain a close bond with my kids, they'll end up hating me and leaving me in a ditch when I'm old?" I quipped.

"Well, yes." She smiled but wouldn't let me use humor to deflect. "That's an extreme example. You haven't told me anything that would indicate you're on a path like that, and there are a lot of steps between having a bad day and your kids hating you."

"I don't want to make a mistake that I'll look back on and say, *That moment right there, that's where I went wrong.* I don't want to lose what I have with them."

"Well, of course. No one does. But what you're doing is predicting. You're spending a lot of time predicting bad things that *could* happen and a lot of time worrying about how that will affect your family, but none of it is really happening." Kim thought this predicting habit was a major driver of my anxiety.

And even though I was powerless to stop it, I knew Kim's assessment was correct. "I'm afraid of dying because of what it would mean for my kids and for Mando."

"Of course. It's very normal to feel vulnerable about death when you're the mom of young kids. You know how much they need you."

Kim provided a moment for this validation to sink in, for me to accept that it was okay—expected, even—to feel scared of this possibility. I cried harder as I said, "They need me so much."

"Yes, they do," she affirmed.

"I think you're right that I'm predicting the worst," I said, after pausing to blow my nose. "My husband's mom died in a car accident when he was sixteen. The whole family was driving home, and someone hit their car right where his mom was sitting." I looked out through the window; the branches whipped outside in the afternoon wind. "Mando's sister, Gina, was only thirteen when her mom died, and I've seen the impact it's had on her. It's like she never recovered. It defined her life."

Becky was a sparkler of a woman who loved and pushed and inspired her two children. Gina needed her, Mando needed her, and after the accident, they were forced to exist without her. Gina was lonely for her mom, and as she got older, her pain seemed to magnify, intensifying when she was confronted with struggles she was forced to navigate alone. When she was diagnosed with lupus—a condition inherited from Becky—it was an additional wound that she couldn't ask her mom for guidance.

For my part, my relationship with Gina was difficult, a field littered with land mines. I tried; I failed; I tried again to love her well. Sometimes the failures were my fault, sometimes they were hers, and some were no one's fault. My efforts, when I did make them, were fumbling and awkward.

I had two close friends—Allie and Kristin—who had grieved the loss of their mothers at different points in their lives. When they both endorsed *Motherless Daughters* as a title that could potentially help Gina process her loss, I was hopeful. I've always found comfort in books, and a love of reading was one of the few things Gina and I connected on. I called to tell her about their recommendation. "My friends said the book is hard to read but worth it. I didn't want to send it without asking, but would you want a copy? I know you'll always miss her, but maybe this could help you address some of the sadness you feel." I was quiet for a moment. "I know it doesn't fix anything. You'll always miss her." I was repeating myself, nervous, concerned about being intrusive.

"I think that could be good," she said, and I mailed the book to her home in Nashville that same day. Though she hadn't pursued therapy (something I'd suggested in the past), perhaps this book would unlock some of her pain, opening up the space for healing that both Mando and I wanted for her.

Mando and I were in Chicago on a kid-free weekend when my phone pinged with the notification that the package had been delivered. A few hours later, Mando's phone lit up with an enraged text from her, accusing me of being insensitive for sending something so triggering.

At the time, this made no sense. Mando's conversations with her became increasingly strained. Accusations were leveled, disappointments recounted. But it wasn't until she started having seizures in the summer of 2017 that we discovered the missing piece: she had been self-medicating her pain with alcohol, and the disorder had spun out of her control.

Gina went to rehab for one day before signing her name on the release to leave the outpatient program. Her husband drove her home without looking back. She assured us she didn't need the treatment.

She began drinking again, but with all the states between us, it was easy to hide.

It wasn't until months later, in the early days of 2018—when Gina and her husband were hospitalized for an infection—that we understood they were both struggling with substance use disorders. Her husband's recovery was straightforward, but Gina's was not. She spent the spring in and out of the hospital in Nashville.

On the day I sat on Kim's couch, Gina was, again, in a hospital bed—and her situation was growing steadily worse. As I was nervously baby-stepping my way through each day, there was a real question whether Gina would ever be well enough to come home from the hospital. She was thirty-four years old.

Gina's trajectory presented a concrete example of one of my greatest fears. In my mind—particularly in my anxious mind—I could trace the line back to a single event. I believed all of her tragedies stemmed from losing her mother.

I looked up at Kim. Her kind face was full of compassion as she responded to my stories about Gina, about the parallels I drew. "It makes sense that the possibility of dying would feel scarier for you," she said gently.

I nodded. "As I get older, I feel this growing sadness for Mando's mom, too, for what she missed out on after she died. I just read Kelly Corrigan's book *Tell Me More*, and she writes about the friend she lost to cancer. The friend had a dream about being in heaven with the other mothers who had to leave early—that was how the friend put it. I don't want to have to leave early."

Kim nodded. It turned out she, too, was a reader. "That's valid," she said. Her tone was sympathetic. "We feel a lot of responsibility to our children, especially when they're young."

As we wrapped up our session, I told Kim about my appointment with Tim and about how I'd experienced new lows after my first visit with her.

She validated this experience: "Beginning therapy can bring up a lot of emotion." Kim's unflappability was a comfort, making me feel like my downturns and drops were to be an expected, even necessary, part of the process.

"I'm glad you started the Zoloft," Kim continued. "I have a lot of patients who find medication helps them." She knew I was looking for approval. Her support was a comfort after the endless second-guessing.

Sometimes it felt like all that stood between my children and tragedy was me, as if I alone held up the galaxy around them. But I wasn't solely responsible for my children's well-being—it's true that it takes a village. I hoped my children would feel the support and love of many people throughout their lives and that they would accept and appreciate that care. Gina struggled many times over to find someone to mother her, to dress her wounds, and set her back upright after a fall.

If I wanted to recover, I knew I had to do the opposite. I would do everything I could to let myself be cared for. I clung to Kim's encouragements. I listened to her voice until I could hear my own again.

19

M Y MOM OCCASIONALLY ASKS ME to tell her the ending of a book.

"Julie, I just want to know: does he survive or what?" she asks, a slightly shrill, annoyed note in her voice. "I raised you! I was in labor with you for twenty hours. The least you can do is tell me this!"

And I smile and say, with saccharine sweetness, "You have to read it yourself."

"Ugh," she responds, disappointed in my uselessness. "*Fine*. I'll ask your sister."

So then, of course, I text Amy and tell her to keep it zipped.

But mirror, mirror on the wall, I am my mother after all. I may not want to know the ending of a book, but I want to know that my story will have a happy ending.

My mom once told me that she wished she could bottle every age as I grew up. I understand this now. I'll look back at photos of

Nolan as a baby and wish that I could hold him and feel his soft, squishy arms. I'm certain I'd enjoy it even more with the benefit of knowing he'd eventually sleep through the night, that he'd learn to walk, that he wouldn't develop weird attachment issues from taking naps snuggled against my chest instead of in the crib. I fretted often when Nolan was a baby.

When Eli was born, the postpartum experience was blissful in comparison. It was helpful that Eli was a thumb-sucker who logged twelve consecutive hours a night by eight weeks and was content to watch in delight as Nolan buzzed around him like a chatty little helicopter. I was more relaxed, less worried, less of a stress case about every tiny thing. I laughed more often when Eli was a baby, and it was a relief.

During the first few years of Eli's life, we had a playroom on the sunny side of our Seattle house. One afternoon when they were both toddlers, my mom and I sat on the floor as the boys played in their child-sized kitchen. They served me imaginary concoctions in their miniature Tupperware cups, promising they would be delicious. I pretended to taste a small sample and then dramatically spit it out, declaring it to be disgusting. "Gross! Ew! Blech! How could you feed this to me?" I'd say, playing the part of the indignant customer. The boys cackled every time, their faces beaming with joy. Making them laugh was—and still is—one of my favorite things. As she would on many other occasions, my mom gazed at the boys' faces, illuminated by the sunshine. She had watched me grow through the first few years of mother-hood, and she felt relieved to see me settling into it. It was a perfect moment, and she knew it as well as I did. "Oh, Julie," she said, "these are your good old days." She was right.

. . .

When Nolan was about seven months old, I had a friend over to our house. As best I can recall, her boys were around eight and ten. I remember only that they seemed massive and dirty and moved around my precious, tiny son like unpredictable frat boys after a few Red Bull vodka cocktails. They were loud. When they ran, their feet pounded the wood floors with slaps that made me flinch. They tried to pick up Nolan and I nearly had a heart attack. After they left, I settled Nolan down for a nap before lying down myself, a Victorian lady taking to her fainting couch after glimpsing her future.

I couldn't have guessed how much I would love being a mom to big boys. I love when sentences start with *dude* or *bruh*. I love sharing edgy humor with them, love watching *Saturday Night Live* together. I love it just as much as I loved those early days. These, too, are good old days.

But they're also bittersweet. When I look at Nolan cracking up as we watch *SNL*, or Eli's huge feet resting on my lap, the joy of the moment is intertwined with the memory of the sun-soaked afternoon in the playroom when I was their everything. These days, like those days, will end. There's a tiny seed of grief embedded in every joy.

In my next session with Kim, I told her, "I've been thinking a lot about that midmom crisis you mentioned, and I think you're reading me correctly. I'm worried that it's going to be a mess from here on out. Nolan's about to go to middle school, and I don't want him getting in with the wrong friends or not talking to us like he does now. I don't want to lose the closeness we have." I didn't want my best days to be behind me, didn't want my good old days to come to an end without my knowledge or explicit permission. And Kim was slowly showing me that my anxiety around the passage of time was tied to the lack of control I felt. I had no way of flipping ahead to the ending, no way of knowing for sure that things would turn out well.

My desire for omniscience extended past the boys, of course. I wanted to fast-forward through the uncertainty of my father's ongoing health scare in Japan, to be reassured that his heart was working as it should. I wanted to move through Gina's crisis. I wanted to know that, in the end, everything would be fine.

Kim worked to bring me back into the present moment, to deal with what was instead of what could be. "Everything you've told me so far demonstrates to me that you have open communication with your kids and husband. You're setting things up as best you can," Kim responded. Her tone became careful. "But you can't know the future."

"I know. But sometimes I wish I could."

20

I'VE ALWAYS LOVED JIGSAW PUZZLES. It had been years since I had completed one at our house because no one else enjoyed them. When I returned to work and time became even tighter, my hobbies were the first, most logical item to place on the chopping block. Plus, Mando got peeved when a puzzle sat out on the table for too long.

I didn't hurry home after finishing my appointment with Kim that afternoon. Instead, I walked down Main Street, watching other people from a distance, all of us anonymous extras in the scene of a movie. Two cyclists zipped by, their neon jerseys painfully bright in the hour before the sunlight downshifted to softer golden. A couple walked by on the opposite side of the street, holding hands and laughing. I fought flashes of envy and shame over the fact that these people seemed to be functioning well, whereas I was counting the days between my appointments with Kim and marking the hours between my doses of Zoloft. I passed flirting high school students and two old men talking on a bench before I reached the blue scalloped awning of the hardware store.

The bell above the door jangled as I entered. I browsed the spinning rack of puzzles in the center aisle of the hardware store, surrounded by an eclectic offering of grills, screws, lawn decor, and little red wagons. When I'd first told my friend Cathie I was struggling, she'd said, "Julie, you need to figure out what brings you joy." It was painfully obvious. When had I stopped doing things that made me happy simply because they made me happy?

I had shared this dawning realization with Kim. "I've neglected myself," I told her, "but it's been convenient for everyone else, so no one has thought to stop me."

A puzzle seemed like a good first step in the right direction. It was an expression of my need to mark out some space for myself—both literally and figuratively. A puzzle would simultaneously slow me down and keep my mind busy, a small distraction to help my brain break the habit of predicting doom everywhere.

I chose a thousand-piece puzzle with pictures of cereal boxes that I recognized from childhood: Cap'n Crunch, Cheerios, Count Chocula. I handed the older gentleman behind the counter my American Express as he attempted to drum up amiable conversation with me, commenting on the weather and asking if I had plans for the evening.

"Just this," I said dryly, gesturing to the puzzle.

"Ha!" He laughed, and I smiled weakly at his generosity. I thanked him before making my way back out onto the Main Street movie set, where I acted as if I, like all these other extras, were doing okay.

. . .

When Eli was two, our brand-new pediatric ophthalmologist told us that he would need eyeglasses.

In the dark exam room with a mural of the ocean on the wall, Eli dug through a pirate's chest of prizes while the ophthalmologist explained Eli's eyes to me. I learned that his vision was compromised because, in addition to a few other conditions, one eye worked harder than the other. Eli's developing brain, even at age two, had already begun making accommodations to compensate for the imbalanced messages coming from the individual eyes. On the first day he had his glasses, in fact, the nurse informed us that for at least a day, although he would be seeing clearly, he would see the world as crooked until his brain stopped performing this rebalancing. I have a vivid memory of him pulling to the left when we arrived at the park later that day, his body doing its utmost to reach the fish slide in one of our favorite parks edging the Puget Sound. Nolan took his hand and helped him forward.

Owing to the early diagnosis and because Eli wore his glasses consistently, we were able to avoid what I've been told is one of the less-pleasant experiences for young children with glasses: patching. For some kids, especially those who don't have intervention until later, the brain adjusts for so long that it begins to rely solely on the stronger eye. Patching is the process of breaking this cycle. The stronger eye is covered, forcing the brain to choose the image from the weaker eye, thus reestablishing (and, it's hoped, strengthening) the connection. The ophthalmologist's office had to work hard at selling this. They even created a wall of "Patch Superstars" filled with photographs of ill-tempered little pirates that I'm sure fooled zero kids into thinking patching would be a super-fun time.

The brain is a machine. It's finely tuned and beautifully complicated, but it prizes efficiency, and so it prefers to follow well-worn routes. I had closed down the paths that connected me to joy, and my brain had readily accepted these losses, growing accustomed before I realized what was happening. Reading books, working on jigsaw puzzles, writing, turning my face to the sun, creating pleasure and leisure, making space for doing nothing: I neglected all these connections when I returned to work in the library.

I believed that I would be most fulfilled by being indispensable, that I was loved because I was needed. Protecting space for ourselves may be an issue for those around us, those who are accustomed to our endless availability. But it's an act of self-care, of self-love, to say, "No, this space—this time—belongs to me."

Later that evening, I sat on the floor and opened up my puzzle, intentionally ignoring the needs around me. Laundry was left in the basket; a messy pile of mail sat on the bench by the front door. I thought back to completing a puzzle with my mom in Seattle years earlier. As we worked to place pieces, my mom yawned. I looked up at the clock and found it was past ten. But we were close to the end, so I lobbied that we should stay up to finish it. I began to place the pieces faster, furrowing my brow as I examined the colors and shapes. My mom sat back and yawned again. She paused to look at me before declaring, matter-of-factly, "Julie, you really know how to suck the joy out of this."

This time, I was aiming to keep the joy intact, which would require moving more slowly. I removed the plastic shrink wrap from the exterior of the yellow box and started to sort out the edge pieces, grouping them by color. Mando turned on *Million Dollar Listing* and set a small glass of wine on the coffee table next to me.

It felt foreign and even a little awkward to work at something intentionally unproductive. But as I sat there, feeling like shit and assembling my puzzle, it occurred to me that I was patching. I was trying to reconnect to joy.

21

I WOKE EARLY ON A Wednesday, which I now thought of as a Kim day. *Five more days to Kim, six days on Zoloft, three more days to Kim, twenty days to go until a month of meds:* my days were measured out not in coffee spoons but in tiny steps toward recovery.

I burrowed down into the nest of my bed for a few additional minutes after silencing the alarm, tucking the covers tightly around my body. I let my eyes adjust to the morning light peeking through the closed shutters as I waited for my phone to power on.

Though I'd seen signs of progress in the past few weeks, I still felt raw, sensitive, and exposed. Mando was trying to muscle through a heavy travel schedule, the typical end-of-the-school-year busyness was upon us, and the load was wrapped with worry about Gina and my dad.

Eli had turned nine on Sunday, and we'd taken some of his friends to see *Avengers: Infinity War.* I'd worried whether the movie was age appropriate, but I hadn't imagined that I'd be the one forced to flee to the ladies' room to pull myself out of a fictional world of death and destruction that felt too real. People could *fly* to imaginary planets in this film, and yet I stood at the sink washing my hands and whispering to myself, using the same self-talk I modeled to the kids at school: "This movie isn't real."

And, of course, my baby was growing older, time passing mercilessly. Seemingly overnight, *Peppa Pig* had been eclipsed by the Marvel universe.

Kim had given me a word for events and moments like this—*triggers*—a now commonplace term that had yet to hit its heyday. Terms like this were one of Kim's early gifts to me. Defining what I was feeling—and why—was the beginning of feeling a semblance of control.

I could quickly begin to identify the triggers in my own life. Reading had slid away from me as the margins of time in my life had grown thinner. But in the past months I'd also noticed that when I did find time to read, many books—ones that my friends loved and highly recommended—were "too much" for me. Chloe Benjamin's *The Immortalists*, in which four siblings know the date of their death, had me spinning for days. Time and anxiety had whittled my reading list down to nothing. (Things are dark when *The Berenstain Bears and Too Much Pressure* feels stressful—my eyes welled up when Mama Bear had a crying meltdown on her bed because the family's schedule was too packed.)

That morning, under the covers, I wasn't thinking about triggers. I tapped the Instagram icon on the screen of my phone and began to scroll through snaps of cute babies, senior pictures of the soon-to-be graduates, spring vacations. I slid past inspirational quotes in hand-lettered cursive, reminding me to be kind or mindful. I watched a parade of people from past and present make their way through my feed, a jumbled history of the many stories—beginnings, middles, ends—nested inside our lives like *matryoshka* dolls.

I paused on a beautiful mountain shot before swiping to see the rest of the carousel of photos. The last picture in the series was a selfie of two women, their heads tilted together with broad smiles, a Pacific Northwest valley as their backdrop, the trees behind them carpeting the hillsides with deep green.

The image was beautiful—and a trigger.

I looked at the smiling blond woman—Casey—on the right, and instantly, my anxiety began to rev. Adrenaline pumped through my limbs. Casey's husband was a coworker of Mando's from our days in Seattle. He'd died suddenly only months before the photo was taken.

The photo on my device shouted its direct, awful message: *sometimes the worst happens.*

Erik was a colleague of Mando's whom we'd known since the beginning of our marriage. He was a good man who worked hard, loved his family. He was a runner—driven, focused, the poster child for health. He woke on a Saturday morning in August of 2017, completed a six-mile run, and attended his daughter's soccer game. But only a few minutes into the game, he sat down on the matted grass of the sidelines, complaining of an intense headache. Casey took him to urgent care, which led them to the ER, which revealed a mass in his brain. Only hours later, during an MRI, blood vessels in the area of the mass ruptured, and he slid into a coma. Four days later, he was gone, his mass a result of a condition that impacts only 1 percent of the population.

After his death, Casey found strength and support by posting about their impossible new normal. She wrote of the brutality of her grief, the steps she was taking to cope. She occasionally posted old videos of Erik laughing or smiling with their two young children. These posts left me gutted. Each time I read or watched one, I'd be pulled from my current moment and dropped into a pit of ache. I ached with her, for her, for the stupid senselessness of the loss. Casey had lost her husband and best friend. It seemed like more than anyone should have to bear. And yet here she was, bearing it. Here we were, in this fragile existence with these mortal loves.

My eyes now burning with tears, I put down the phone, forced myself out of the cocoon of my bed, and stumbled into an uphill climb of a day that, post-trigger, had become steeper.

That afternoon, Kim and I discussed the unavoidable triggers strewn throughout my days. I told her about my dentist appointment on Monday. While getting a cavity filled, I'd gripped the pleather beige armrests of the chair so aggressively that my hands had ached for hours after the Novocain had worn off.

"Triggers can be powerful, especially when you're learning to identify them. And you're definitely not the only one who feels that way about the dentist," she said with a laugh.

I told her about seeing Casey's Instagram. "Every time I see her posts, I feel a wave of sadness. And I also feel scared that something could happen to Mando." I paused before continuing. "I think that's the predicting we talked about."

"Yes. It sounds like you feel deeply for Casey and also identify with her."

I nodded. Because it was so near, so *possible*, Erik's death had left a wound. And though I'd tried to ignore it, it demanded attention. "I think maybe I need to adjust my settings so Casey's posts don't pop up when I'm not expecting them." I'd resisted making that change for months, telling myself it was selfish to block out someone else's pain. But it was no longer a question of selfishness: I simply couldn't handle it.

"I don't want to put their family out of my mind like it's not happening, because it is. But maybe I can remove the element of surprise. I need to control the timing because they impact me so deeply."

We were quiet for a moment before Kim said gently, "I think changing those post settings might be a kind thing to do for yourself."

"I hate that I can't handle anything right now," I admitted. I was accustomed to supporting others, and now I could barely handle myself.

"This is just where you are right now," Kim said.

I looked up from the pile of tissues in my lap. "I'm so fragile."

"Yes," she said, nodding. She leaned forward slightly in her chair, made careful eye contact. "But remember, Julie, fragile doesn't mean broken."

22

MEMORIAL DAY AT THE POOL was sold to me as "a family day" by my husband.

I sat at the edge of the pool at our friends' country club, watching my children splash happily in the water, the sun bronzing their shoulders. Though it was late May, it was only warm in the direct sun, still glacial in the shade. I wore a forest-green North Face fleece, zipped up all the way, as I hunched on a couch under a cabana, surrounded by three other women—Allie, Kristin, and a friend of Kristin's who was barely an acquaintance to me. Dark sunglasses hid my tired eyes. I hadn't even considered swimming. The brightness of the sunshine reflected off the bleached walls of the Spanish-styled buildings in a way that further irritated me, as if the glare was personally directed at me. Our husbands were playing golf. Apparently the "family" part would happen when they returned to share lunch with us.

I was angry.

I had nothing to offer that day. I was empty. I had no easy

conversation, no ability to feign interest, no manners or social skills. I tucked myself into the corner of the outdoor sectional and retreated into the hood of my jacket like an angry turtle.

I'd spoken to Kristin and Allie after my visit with Tim, when I had finally had words to tell them why I seemed to be a different person than the Julie they knew. They looked at me from the other side of the sectional with compassion and uncertainty.

I'd met the other woman in our group only in passing at a baseball game. Perhaps, on a different day, I would've felt more tolerant of her steady stream of mindless chatter, but on that Memorial Day, I had no patience for anyone.

"I wore long sleeves today because I have this *thing* on my arm and it's *so gross*," she said. Her horror was so pronounced that I felt misled when she pulled up her sleeve to reveal a small, insignificant spot of what resembled eczema. She perched on the edge of the couch, her Gucci sunglasses sitting on top of her head, her Louis Vuitton bag slung casually on the couch between us. "Anyway, Kristin, I know I started to tell you this the other day, but last week Sam brought his new boss to our house in the middle of the morning. No text, no heads-up, so I met him for the first time *in my workout clothes*."

Though Allie and Kristin laughed politely, I scowled and pulled further into my shell. I was beyond caring whether this woman would walk away and think, *Wow. Julie is a horrible bitch.* My frustration overwhelmed me. Why was I making small talk when I hate small talk? Why was I sitting on this couch like a glorified babysitter while Mando golfed? After the past few months, why had either of us thought this would be a good idea for today?

I should've said it loudly and clearly that morning: "I'm not up for this." But I didn't know how to do it, and Mando didn't know how to do it for me.

Just as my anger was reaching its peak, we saw the dads crest the hill, descending the stairs that led down to the pool deck. They looked relaxed and sun-kissed. The four of them were straight out of a Titleist ad campaign for premium golf balls.

Mando stepped up and hugged me, a broad smile on his face. He was happy and initially missed—or chose to ignore—my tight body language and my short, clipped responses to his questions.

I asked him about his golf game with a flat, perfunctory "How'd you play?"

He responded with an enthusiastic "Good! I played well on the back nine. How'd things go here?"

"Oh, super fun. We're just sitting here supervising the children while you guys live your best lives." My words oozed sarcasm, but Mando laughed good-naturedly and put his arm around my waist, planting a kiss on my cheek as the country club server arrived with a round of beers for the guys. She passed out the drinks with a broad smile, tipping her Wayfarers onto her head as she tucked the empty tray under her arm. We navigated the painful process of ordering food with a large group, and she departed.

"Cornhole," said one of the guys, and just like that, they disappeared again, walking across the deck into the sun, laughing as they decided the teams. The moms and I slank back to our shady prison and managed the increasingly frequent visits of the soggy children, who were now wet *and* hungry. Thirty minutes dripped by. My mood did nothing for the vibe.

By the time the food arrived, I was practically vibrating with fury, sending vengeful telepathic waves across the pool at Mando as he laughed and sipped his beer. I was depleted. I was tired of feeling awful and tired of pretending I didn't feel awful. I was lonely and desperate. I felt trapped in my body and this sick joke of a family day.

The food arrived and the men sauntered over to collect their lunch, casually grabbing pieces of sandwiches and handfuls of french fries before returning to the other side of the pool to continue their game.

Viewed from the outside, the situation was idyllic. I was sitting at a country club, for goodness' sake. Someone was preparing and serving food to my family, all of whom were healthy and happy. I was among friends and could've been sipping a mimosa, had I chosen to. On the surface, there was nothing I could possibly complain about.

But my heart ached precisely because I knew this to be true. I was incapable of enjoying these pleasures, and that realization rocked me. Regardless of the setting, there was no escaping *me*. Standing outside of my life was painful. I knew I was missing out, and yet there was nothing I could do to reengage, to step back in. The helplessness was salt in the wound.

When Mando bent down to grab his beer, he quietly asked me if I was okay. It felt like lip service, because anyone could tell that I was not.

"No," I said flatly. "I'm done here. I need to go home."

"Okay," he replied casually, "we'll head out soon." The other dads were calling to him from the other side of the pool and he left, jogging a little so as not to delay the game. *Wouldn't want to inconvenience the guys*, I thought acidly.

I waited about fifteen minutes before I texted Mando from my spot on the sectional: Let's go.

His response came to my phone ten minutes later. Yes. I'll finish this and then we're out!

I listened to the dads' laughter and clenched my teeth.

I waited ten more long minutes before I sent a sarcastic text: Take your time over there. Then, five minutes later, LET'S GO.

I saw Mando reach for his phone, and I watched his jaw twitch as he read my texts. He tucked his phone into his pocket, bid the other husbands goodbye, and walked over to me. I could tell by his gait that he was angry. He walked over and started picking up towels, then stood in front of me and said, "Let's go."

Kristin hugged me. "Ugh, you shouldn't have come," she said quietly, her Boston directness getting straight to the ugly truth of the moment, her love softening it. Kristin understood that this day had been a spectacularly bad idea. How could she see this so clearly when Mando could not? Allie hugged me goodbye and told me she loved me, squeezing my shoulders in a quick validating acknowledgment. I said a hasty goodbye to the other woman and followed Mando, who was already climbing the stairs to leave the pool area. He was opening the trunk when I caught up with him at the car.

I began to cry when I saw his face, the hardness in his eyes. We got in the car and the children were silent, picking up on our tension. I whispered to Mando, "Why are you doing this?"

"What? You wanted to leave. We're leaving." He squeezed the steering wheel as he backed out of the parking spot. We drove home in silence, and I looked out the window, wiping my tears in an attempt to hide them from the boys. The air in the car was heavy with emotion and recrimination and misunderstanding. I watched the landscape slip by and felt terribly, awfully alone.

Before I experienced my first migraine, shortly after Nolan was born, I had assumed that migraines were simply severe headaches. But after vomiting on the way to urgent care and receiving an injection in the left butt cheek, I became quickly, painfully aware of the difference. We don't know what we don't know.

And in the same way, before the spring of 2018, I thought that anxiety was a term for severe worrying. I had it cataloged as a problem for the irrational, the unreasonable, the overly sensitive. I considered anxiety to be a matter of choice and control, as if a good workout and some simple paradigm shifts would help someone "snap out of it." Oh, what I didn't know.

Having spent half my life with him, I knew—*knew*—that's what Mando was thinking as he sat beside me in the driver's seat, fuming. He was annoyed with my weakness because he mistakenly believed I was choosing to wallow, that I was allowing myself to stay stuck.

My loneliness hardened into angry resolve as we drove across town. Mando had no concept of what I was experiencing, no clue as to the depth of my suffering on that sunny day. My anxiety was a metaphorical migraine, but Mando was convinced I had only a bad headache.

Mando pulled into the driveway and put the car in park as I issued instructions to the kids. "Pop your suits and towels into the washer and then get in the shower, boys." They hustled out of the car and headed inside without a word of argument, their radar tracking the dark clouds gathering between their parents. I stood next to Mando as he unloaded the car. He pointedly ignored me. I heard the door to the house swing closed behind us.

"What?" He shot the word like a starting gun, marking the official beginning of our argument.

"I don't understand why you're the one who's mad," I began.

"Julie, you sent me an all-caps text, and suddenly we have to leave. I don't get it. We were all having fun hanging out."

"No, we weren't having fun. You were having fun. You and the other dads, while the moms were stuck watching the kids."

Perhaps The Ideal Woman wouldn't complain about supervising the children while her husband played golf, but I was tired of playing that role. Something in me had snapped.

Mando shook his head as he picked up the cooler, turning his body to place the red monstrosity under the workbench in the garage. I waited for him to turn around.

"Whatever," he said. He slammed the trunk and walked over to empty his golf bag. I took a few steps toward him because I wasn't finished with the conversation. It felt good to stand up for myself, and I refused to back down.

"Mando, why are *you* angry? I told you I needed to leave. I told you more than once and you put me off because you were having a grand old time playing cornhole!"

He shook his head as he knocked some of the grass off his golf shoes. "I don't get it. We were just *hanging out.*"

"Yes!" I shrieked a little as I said it. "But I can't do that right now! I sat there listening to Kristin's friend telling us about bullshit problems that aren't even problems, and I wanted to come home. I was *done.* We were there for *six hours!*"

He continued to shake his head as he wiped off his golf clubs and slipped on the covers. He zipped his glove into the side pocket and picked up the bag before placing it next to the water heater. He was silent, unmoved.

"Mando, I told you I needed to leave, and you ignored me."

He looked at me, his face tight. I saw that he wasn't ready to back down either, that he clung to the assumption that my desperation to leave was driven by selfishness or a need for control.

I knew he was wrong, which was why I wouldn't apologize for my rude texts, wouldn't apologize for feeling angry that he'd put his own happiness above my needs that day. But I was wrung out and couldn't argue anymore. I looked at him and shook my head. "I'm already suffering here, and this, you being so hard on me, *because* I'm suffering? You're hurting me. You're making it worse." Hot, angry tears sprang from my eyes as I walked into the house.

I took a shower to wash off the day, to scrub away the film of frustration and resentment that covered my skin. As the hot water beat down on my back, I whispered to myself: *I will not apologize.* I girded my determination as I aggressively shampooed my scalp. I hated leaving things unsettled with Mando, but I wouldn't capitulate just to end the argument. I had asked for care—I had said it out loud—and Mando should've heard and responded. I wasn't asking too much.

Memorial Day was the day I stopped apologizing for my needs.

Later, Mando and I stood in the kitchen, the island between us, a literal representation of the distance we both felt. We stood at opposite ends of the same mess, both of us angry and broken-hearted. But I was calm and resolute.

"Mando, I hate being in this place. I *hate* it. But all I can do is wait. And I've got to be able to ask you for a rescue and know that you'll hear me."

He, too, had calmed down. "I know," he said with a resigned sigh. "I know." He hated it too.

"I can't feel alone in this."

"I know," he said, opening his arms. And we both took steps to close the distance, to embrace, to become an island—the two of us, waiting together for the rescue.

23

MANDO AND I HAD PATCHED up things, but my anger remained close to the surface until I sat down on Kim's brown couch the following Wednesday.

"I feel like Mando's complicit in this," I began.

"In what, specifically?"

"In my depletion. The depression might be connected to my chemistry, but I'm also overextended because I do so much." I stopped myself, feeling the sudden need to backtrack out of loyalty to my husband. "I mean, it isn't his *fault*," I said. Despite my frustration, I didn't want her to have the wrong idea about Mando.

"Well, no, of course not. But is it yours?"

"I don't think so," I began, but I was hesitant. Over the years, we'd developed a dynamic in which I took care of nearly everything that wasn't work-related. The imbalance was only exacerbated by Mando's increasingly frequent travel. Often, I took care of challenges at home without his involvement because there was literally nothing he could do to help from the road. Sometimes I even forgot to tell him. Who can possibly recount an entire day with children, the thousands of conversations and battles that can be launched and fought and resolved in twelve short hours? I explained all this to Kim and tried to make sense of how this invisible work factored into my burnout. "I feel like I've stopped telling him what I need, and he's stopped asking," I said, looking up from my hands. "Hence the Memorial Day situation. I finally asked, and he didn't respond the way I wanted him to."

I craved no one's respect more than Mando's, but over the years, as I'd worked to show him how competent I was, he'd become accustomed to me taking care of the details of our life. I'd strived to be seen as capable—strong, unflappable, efficient—and I had stopped telling him when the daily grind was hard or taxing. And because I was the one with too many feelings in our marriage and he was the one with too few, I had long since stopped telling him about situations that were emotional. But because I kept all those feelings bottled, I had no one to tell me to slow down or take a break or do *less*.

In Mando's defense, my desire to speak about my inner life had surged back with a justifiable but shocking vengeance. It had caught him off guard. My emotions, my needs, my anxious mental state—none of which would've been his topic of choice to begin with—were now sloppily mixed and prepared as a wilted amuse-bouche for every conversational meal.

Kim counseled grace for the both of us. We were out of practice in talking this way, she emphasized. She asked what we were doing to nourish our relationship.

I paused. I knew Mando was my person, but we'd put little to no effort into our connection for the past few months. "I'm worried we might drift apart. Like our sex life, which has always been great, feels like it's on pause right now," I said, forcing myself to share something that felt personal and tender. "I don't like it. I worry that we'll lose that part of our intimacy."

Kim gently mentioned that this sounded a lot like predicting. "Julie, it sounds like you and Mando have a very solid foundation."

"We do," I conceded. We'd been together since we were nineteen, but we'd been lucky to grow together as we'd grown up.

"Then what if you could trust what you've built? Trust that you and Mando can handle this lull and that when you're feeling better things will get back on track?"

I laughed as I nodded. "The slowdown isn't exactly a mystery, I guess, considering I'm exhausted and insanely emotional," I said. I gestured to my face, my puffy eyes, my congested sinuses. "Who wouldn't want to hit this?"

She laughed a little. "You don't have to worry about why it's not happening right now because you understand it," she continued. "And you don't need to forecast that this dry spell will continue. You can recognize your pattern of predicting the worst-case scenario."

I nodded. I noticed that I felt much calmer for having voiced my fear to Kim. Putting words to my feelings was a relief, and I was doing it more and more often with her. Perhaps she was right in her suggestion that I wasn't on a direct path to becoming a shriveled-up prude with a cobwebbed vagina.

On the drive home, I pictured myself carrying a heavy back-pack of worry rocks, each with its own little label, its own ugly scenario. Kim had given me permission to toss one rock to the side of the road. And if I could do that with the first rock, maybe there were others I could drop too.

24

THE LAST DAY OF SCHOOL before summer vacation arrived like the end of a long road trip—a slog of hours until suddenly, we pulled into the driveway. There had been signs of progress in the last month of school. I'd been able to eat a little more, rest a little more, *feel* a little more. But some old habits were hard to break.

And at the top of that list: saying yes when I didn't truly *want*—and even worse, *need*—to do something. The habit led to a tight little cycle:

> *Say yes* ➡ *Feel pissed at myself for saying yes* ➡
> *Justify the yes by classifying a no as selfish* ➡
> *Feel overwhelmed* ➡ *Muscle through the*
> *obligation because I said yes in the first place*

It was Nolan's last day of elementary school, and that morning, he and his class visited me in the library for the last time, returning their books at my desk. I had deep, complicated feelings about this change, but as Kim had counseled me to do, I let those feelings come and go.

"Good luck in the assembly, Mom," Nolan said as he headed out into the hallway. I felt my stomach drop at the reminder.

I'd agreed to participate in an optional—optional!—dance routine with some of the staff for the last day of school assembly. As soon as I'd clicked yes on the request sent from the teacher organizing the group, a former Raiderette, I knew it was the wrong choice. Should a middle-aged depressed woman who's clinging to the shreds of herself learn and perform a dance on what promises to be an already emotional day? Clearly, the answer was no, but I'd said yes, and now I was committed and therefore slogging miserably through the cycle of regret. I followed my colleague's video instructions for days to learn the routine cho-reographed to—oh, the irony—Pharrell Williams's "Happy." I cursed myself every time I set my phone up on my dresser before spending twenty minutes parroting the moves, a frown pasted on my face as I half-assed my way through.

And that's how I ended up dancing like a sad, awkward mari-onette in front of eight hundred elementary school students. Though I was clearly an unsettling vision for these impres-sionable minds, though I was waiting for the Zoloft to kick in, though I was inching my way through each day, I still managed to think I *should*.

I made it through, returned to the edges of the gym, and vowed to learn my lesson. I would say yes only to things I *wanted* to do. I would add a pause between the ask and the response, one that would allow me to think slightly more critically about the shape of my days. But it was the sort of lesson that takes extra time and patience to master.

The idea that you say yes only if you truly *want* to do something sounds straightforward and, frankly, wonderful, but any woman will tell you it's not quite that simple.

Later that day, I stood behind the semicircle of my desk, drained but proud. The school was empty of students and the library was ready for summer. The rainbow carpet was rolled up and set to the side. The chairs hung upside down off the shelves to allow for the floors to be cleaned. The counters were clear, the computers unplugged, the paperwork in order. The sixteen thousand books were all in their proper places (or close enough—I'd been following my mom's recent advice to cut corners when I could).

I listened to music as I purged and cleaned and sorted. A new Panic! at the Disco song came on, its catchy beat reaching me through my fog, and I snorted as I registered the title—"High Hopes." Then I turned it up, enjoying the sweet rebellion of listening to loud music at school. By the final chorus, I surprised myself by even singing along a bit. How long had it been since I'd enjoyed music? For three minutes and eleven seconds, I felt a weak ray of joy break through the clouds.

Not quite happy, not quite high hopes, but it was enough.

25

EVEN WHEN I'M NOT DEPRESSED, I hate indoor trampoline parks. They're dangerous germ fests that smell like feet. And yet, thanks to another ill-advised yes, I found myself spending a beautiful June day inside one with Kristin, Allie, and the kids on the boys' swim team.

The walls of the trampoline park just across the freeway were offensively bright, painted in garish orange and neon green. We paid an exorbitant amount for entry, and then the boys shoved their feet into their new grippy socks. The teenage employee with the long ponytail stepped over to wrap their wrists with color-coded bands; they thanked her hastily before shooting off in all directions. I smiled at her and then walked over to sit with Kristin and Allie, who waited for me at a table next to the food court.

The shouts of children echoed in the cavernous space. I performed a quick check-in with myself and was surprised to find that I felt generally okay despite all of this. It was a new practice: I would check in often, paying attention to my moods, triggers, and feelings. My baseline was stabilizing as a result of the Zoloft and my weekly visits with Kim, but progress was slow. I was still terribly sensitive and triggered by pretty much everything. The world offers no shortage of things to worry about.

Allie and Kristin stood to hug me as I walked over to the cheap laminated table. Allie had chauffeured the kids to swim practice for me over the last week so I could tie up loose ends in the library—she'd offered, and I'd gratefully accepted her help.

"Thanks again for covering with the kids," I said as I sat down on the uncomfortable plastic chair. The table was sticky and strewn with mysterious crumbs; I hung my purse on the back of the chair and tried not to touch anything. "It was great to have that time to purge a bunch of crap I haven't touched for a year." Allie and I shared a love of getting rid of stuff. She'd donated so much of her wardrobe that once, when she asked her husband if he knew where her jeans were, he said, "Probably at Goodwill, Allison!" For my part, Mando and I had happily tossed some pieces of wood when we moved into our house—and were very sad to later figure out they were custom shelves for our living room built-ins.

"My pleasure," Allie said, smiling. "You know I love throwing away shit."

As we continued our catch-up, Kristin asked about my dad and Allie looked toward me expectantly.

"We don't know anything for sure yet. He finally had his CT scan, and then his doctor referred him to a cardiologist. That's next week. It's moving too slowly, I think, but there doesn't seem to be anything we can do about that." I was oddly calm about the out-of-control situation unfolding an ocean away.

Allie and Kristin let their short exhales speak for them. They both lost their mothers to cancer—Kristin was in her thirties; Allie was only eight. Allie's older sister was diagnosed with breast cancer at thirty-five. They were both well acquainted with scans and understood the agony of waiting, the desperation that drives an attempt to extract meaning from the inscrutable expression on a tech's face.

"That's a lot, Julie," Kristin said.

"Any update on Gina?" Allie asked.

"She's not improving," I said. "They're talking about dialysis. It's bad. Mando's anticipating he'll go to Nashville at some point soon."

My two friends both shook their heads. Then Kristin said, in a low voice, "Not to really bring us down here, but did you guys *hear* about Kate Spade?"

I had not heard anything about Kate Spade because turning off the news had been an early step in Julie's Antianxiety Plan, beginning with deleting *Meet the Press* recordings that still, after all this time, made me miss hearing Tim Russert's voice. In addition to avoiding stressful world news, I'd learned from my Instagram feed that surprises weren't good for me. I was handling what was happening with my dad and Gina, but in both cases, I created windows of time to adjust. Knowing at least a little of what *could* come didn't make it easier, but it did make it less likely that updates would throw me into a panic.

"What about Kate Spade?" I felt myself tense and the anxiety begin to swirl.

"She died by suicide," Kristin said, somber. "She hung herself."

My body was off like a shot. By the time she uttered, "Can

you imagine?" my heart rate was climbing and my chest was tightening.

I turned instinctively to Allie, who looked me straight in the eye, putting her hand on my knee. Kristin's attention was drawn to a new conversation on the other side of the table and Allie said to me, quietly and directly, "That's not going to happen to you."

I nodded and inhaled, attempting to breathe in her words. I blinked away the threat of tears and gazed up at the black trampoline netting and the too-bright fluorescent lights, stared at the vending machines next to the cubbies full of sloppily stowed shoes. I looked around, waiting, grounding myself. *I'm here, I'm okay. I'm here, I'm okay.*

An announcement blared through the space that the next dodgeball game was starting. I glanced at my watch and read 3:30. Only thirty minutes left until we could escape this colorful hellhole. *We'll pick up dinner at Chipotle*, I decided. Mando was out of town.

My breathing slowly returned to normal.

This small, seemingly unimportant recovery was monumental. For the first time in a while, I'd managed to regain my equilibrium, to slide from dysregulation to regulation, helped by my friend's understanding words. And now I was looking for ways to keep the rest of the day simple, absent of striving and shoulds. This new mindset allowed me to make decisions based not on what was *best*, but what was good enough. Sure, salmon with salad and a little fruit was probably best, but considering we had zero of those ingredients at home and the boys gagged extravagantly when lettuce was even placed near their plates, there were plenty of reasons to discard that vision. No dishes, easy pickup, full bellies, and happy children: Chipotle was good enough for that night.

Thirty minutes until we could pick up dinner, five hours until the boys would be in bed, nineteen hours until Mando's plane would touch down in Oakland. Forty-eight hours and thirty minutes until I could go see Kim, sit on her couch, and talk about my persistent fear that my slip would turn into a slide, that the slide wouldn't have a bottom, and that I, too, would feel that to die would be the only way out.

26

Though I'm old enough to know that the world doesn't stop turning simply because I'm in crisis, I was still shocked when my mom called with the news that my dad needed surgery the following week in Japan. I stood frozen in the middle of the kitchen, my hand resting on the island, the boys watching me, awaiting the first break in the conversation to ask me whatever "urgent" question they had in their minds. I waved my hand at them in a sweeping motion, and they gave up, leaving me to sink into a chair to try to absorb what my mom was telling me.

"The cardiologist said your dad's arteries are blocked." I heard her shuffling to find the paper with the exact measurements. "There are four vessels. Three are blocked: Two are 60 percent occluded and the other is 99 percent occluded. The 99 percent one means that he could have been *days* away from a fatal heart attack. Dr. Tanaka said he shouldn't get on a plane."

"Oh, Mom . . ."

My mom was resolutely grateful. "Julie, I'm just so glad they found it," she said. "It's truly a miracle."

I heard Nolan and Eli bickering down the hall and felt murderous at their inability to read the room. "Mom, can we call you back? I'm going to have the boys shower and then we'll FaceTime."

I gritted my teeth as I walked down the hall to issue my commands. The boys knew my clenched jaw and quiet voice meant I was truly on the verge of losing it. I finished with, "Come to the couch after you're showered."

The boys had been counting the weeks until they would see their grandparents, knowing that it came with trips to the LEGO store, Hershey's kisses unwrapped for them, and games of Bullshit, a word that had quickly taken root in their shared lexicon. They plopped down next to me a few minutes later, the last beads of water still clinging to their hair.

"Guys, Mimi and Poppy can't come next week."

Their disappointment was immediate and indignant. "What? Why?"

"Poppy has some stuff happening with his heart, and he has to get it fixed before he can come here. We're going to call him on FaceTime now and talk to him, and we're going to tell him we love him," I coached them. "We're all disappointed, but it's important he gets this fixed."

The phone connected and my dad's face appeared on the screen. He was pale, his face drawn. His wrinkles seemed to stand out more starkly as he sipped his water and my mom hovered nearby. But he was determined. He told us that Dr. Tanaka scheduled two surgeries—one for Monday to address the largest occlusion and a second surgery Wednesday to place the stents in the other two vessels. My mom wasn't happy about these procedures happening in Japan: heart surgery isn't an ideal time to navigate a language barrier and vast cultural differences. But both she and my dad understood there were no other options for treatment when the need was so acute. He couldn't risk a ten-hour plane ride to the West Coast. They reassured me that Dr. Tanaka was well respected in Japan.

I had never hated the distance between us more.

Between the members of my family of origin—my mom, dad, brother, and sister, and I—we've had nearly every surgery under the sun. We've sat in the waiting room for appendectomies, bunion corrections, total knee replacements, tonsillectomies, back surgeries, and a deviated septum. We have a tried-and-true strategy for postrecovery medication: *Stay ahead of the pain.* Part of the strangeness of my sudden anxiety was that historically I had been calm under pressure. All things considered, we're pretty good in a crisis. One summer, when I was home from college, my dad appeared at the screen door between the kitchen and the family room where my siblings and I were watching a movie and generally being useless.

"Hey, Jules, can you grab this door?"

I got up, eyes remaining on the television screen, and slid the door aside for him to pass, pushing it closed behind him without ever breaking my gaze.

He moved to the sink behind us and began washing his hands before saying, in a voice so nonplussed that he could have been commenting on the weather, "I think I'm going to need someone to drive me to the emergency room." He had sliced open his thumb with a hedge trimmer and was bleeding all over the sink, but, naturally, he insisted on a quick shower before we left.

The boys took turns FaceTiming with my parents. They were irreverent and silly, their lightness balancing the heaviness of the day and the news. Watching them, I felt grateful and grounded. I was focusing on my recovery not only for myself but for the people I loved, the people who loved me.

Eli finished first and said goodbye before walking down the hall to brush his teeth. He made it halfway there before turning around and running back toward me, shouting "Poppy!" He pushed his face into the frame. "You know what I think about your heart stuff?"

Dad smiled. "What?" he asked.

"I think it's . . . bullshit," he said with a grin, delighted to get away with a bad word.

"Ha!" My dad barked a loud laugh as he shook his head and said, "You're right, Eli. It's total bullshit."

27

As my dad's situation was occupying our minds, so was Gina's. The day after my conversation with my parents, Mando received a call to tell him that Gina's health had taken a very sharp downturn. Her kidneys were failing, and her body was decompensating rapidly. I sat next to Mando as he booked the flight to Nashville to say goodbye to his sister. Gina had turned thirty-five a few days earlier.

And all I could do was sit next to him, one hand on his back, as he clicked and typed.

"It feels like such a waste," I told Kim. They were hard words, words I couldn't say to Mando or even to a friend, and once again I found myself grateful for the safe space of therapy. But Gina was so young. How could it feel anything but wrong?

"It sounds like she's experienced an inordinate amount of trauma in her life," Kim pointed out.

"She called once, before we found out she was still drinking,"

I said, "and told Mando she was having a panic attack. She said her husband was napping, which we found strange because it was evening—around 7:00 p.m. in Nashville. I couldn't figure out why she would call Mando, who's across the country, when her husband was in the next room. Go wake him up! Her response seemed irrational."

I'd been frustrated with her at the time, wanting her to take the obvious next step to care for herself. I didn't yet understand that anxiety is anything but rational. I assumed she had a headache when she was suffering from a migraine—I didn't know what I didn't know.

"And now you understand," Kim prompted.

"I do, yes. I feel compassion for her, but it's complicated. I've spent a lot of time over the past few years trying to figure her out, and now that I'm getting snatches of insight, it's too late for it. Understanding won't change what's happening right now." I looked out the window and saw the buds and blossoms had fallen, leaving the bright green leaves alone on the trees. "It's like she had two demons devouring her. If the substances weren't consuming her, then the depression was, and they fueled each other. I don't know if it was possible for her to find her way out."

What I wanted was to rewind the timeline and pinpoint the exact moment when Gina's future was cemented. Was it the moment she chose a partner whose weaknesses mirrored hers? Was it when her mom died? Did the loss of Becky have to result in more loss, an exponential expansion of pain?

Gina's choices created frustration and pain for the people who loved her, and so many of those choices pushed her away from the possibility of a healthy future. But who was I to judge the way she coped with the impossible losses in her life? Pain is a devouring, shape-shifting monster that can't be underestimated. She made her choices while under the influence of that pain, and then those choices tumbled into what seemed to be an inescapable cycle.

"I think I try to understand her trajectory because I don't want to make a bunch of choices that have a cumulative effect. Or make a choice that puts me past the point of no return. I don't want to look up and find I'm too far gone," I told Kim.

"Predicting?" Kim pointed out. I nodded. "You said that Gina never went to therapy?"

"No. We encouraged her to find a good therapist so many times."

"Well, you're here, Julie. Your presence shows you're already doing things differently."

I felt a wave of gratitude that I was able to be there, week after week. "I wish she could've done the same," I said, feeling the weight of regret on my heart.

That weekend, before Mando left, we told the boys what was happening in the most basic terms, leaving out the complicated details for the moment. At bedtime, I lay down with Eli and rubbed my hand along his back. It was dark in his room, but when he said my name, I knew his eyes were filled with tears. Though they were brave and loving and resilient, I was tired of having these heavy conversations with the boys.

"Mom," he whispered, "if Gina dies, then Dad will have barely any family left."

I sighed before offering him the only honest comfort I could find. "I know, pal. Thank goodness he has us, right?"

I could feel Eli nod in the dark. I wished I had an explanation for the brutal unfairness of the world. We said a prayer for Mando and then I ran my fingers through Eli's dark, thick hair. I told him I loved him, closing the door quietly before going to Nolan's room to tuck him in and hug him tight.

Mando prepared for his trip in his usual ways. He charged his iPad, he set up his autoresponder on his work email, he shaved and packed his Dopp kit. He was prepared but not ready. There was never any possibility of being ready.

When we went to bed that night, our hands found each other across the expanse of our bed. Our fingers interlocked, and I turned over on my side to place my other hand on top of our joined palms, to hold his hand between mine. I said a prayer of thanks that I felt just stable enough to handle this trip, to not add to his pain.

"I'm sorry," I whispered. The words weren't enough, and my mind searched for other words, flipping through the dictionary in my head in vain. I wanted to say: I'm sorry you have to say good-bye to the girl you've known all your life, one of the only people left who remembered your beautiful mother in the same way you do, the person who spoke the language of your first home, your first life. I wanted to say something that would ease his burden, which was, of course, impossible.

Instead I squeezed his hand, hoping to communicate what I most wanted to say: I'll be here when you get back.

28

As Mando's flight departed for Nashville, my father was rolled into the operating room for heart surgery in Japan. Even for someone who's not in the throes of a mental-health crisis, this sort of day would be easily categorized as "a lot." Though I worried I wouldn't be able to keep it together, I knew it was incredibly important that I do just that, and the importance of that task kept me in the moment. The only way through the day was step by literal step, and mercifully, I was getting pretty good at that.

Mando arrived in Nashville in the late afternoon, the sun burning away the last hours of daylight. His dad picked him up at the airport, and they drove straight to the hospital to spend the evening by Gina's side. By the time he called me that night he was exhausted, fully consumed by travel and grief.

"She doesn't look good," he reported, his voice flat and discouraged.

"I'm so sorry, love," I said gently, "I hate that this is happening. Did you talk to the doctor?"

"We spoke with a few of them. One of the neurologists told us that her last scan showed brain tissue that would be characteristic for a sixty-year-old." I winced. Her body had endured so much: car accidents, trauma, grief, her attempts to self-medicate.

Mando's voice sounded gravelly when he said, "We're going back to the hospital tomorrow morning, and they're thinking we'll remove life support then."

My heart sank. "I love you so much, Mando."

"I love you too." We sat on the line for a moment, taking a pause together. "How's your dad doing?" he asked.

I was relieved to have good news to share on this otherwise dark day. "The surgery was pretty stressful, but it was successful. I guess the doctor came out after an hour and a half and told Mom it wasn't going well, and he needed to know if she wanted him to continue with the catheterization or perform a triple bypass instead." When Dr. Tanaka used a vein in my dad's wrist to gain entry to his network of vessels, he found my dad's physiology to be a twisted, tangled maze with switchbacks that caused the catheter they tried to insert to collapse on itself. "Mom told him to do whatever he felt more comfortable with. He was able to place the stent, but it took four hours." The vessel they'd addressed presented the most acute need. In medical circles, the LAD (left anterior descending) artery is known as the Widowmaker. For my parents, the nickname was very nearly accurate. Now they'd hunker down for recovery before the next surgery.

Next we caught up on the boys. Mando, needing to feel grounded in our lives even from a distance, wanted to know the plans for the following day. "Water World with the swim team," I told him. "It's supposed to be over a hundred degrees, but they're excited, so whatever." Mando knew my feelings about Water World, which were less than positive. A friend had recently told me a childhood story about her sister sliding through another kid's barf on a water slide after the attendant had let them go down too close together. This anecdote had done nothing for my attitude.

"I appreciate you, Julie. I'm sure they'll have a blast."

I could tell he needed sleep. "Go to bed, love."

I set my phone down on the coffee table in front of me and let myself cry. *It's too much*, I thought, *but here we are.*

The following morning, as Mando sat at his sister's bedside in Nashville, I rolled up beach towels and shoved them into a large tote in the laundry room. I tossed goggles into the bag and thought about my mom and dad, stranded in a country where they didn't speak the language at a time when words mattered more than usual. I filled water bottles as I considered Gina's short life, as I conjured alternate pasts that would've created a better future, a happier ending. I spread peanut butter and jelly onto slices of bread. I sandwiched existential musings between the tasks required to get three people on the road for a hot day.

Once inside the water park, we met up with friends and found a tiny square of shade next to a lone palm tree. I released my kids to explore the labyrinth of water slides and lazy rivers while the other mothers and I spent the morning periodically scooting our chairs around the palm tree, chasing the slowly rotating slivers of shadow of the natural sundial. I held my phone in my lap, waiting for a text from Mando. I received his last one just after we arrived: They're going to remove the life support.

I pictured my husband, holding his sister's hand.

Around the two-and-a-half-hour mark at Water World, I'd had enough of eyeing the slides for potential pukers. I realized I needed to get the hell out of there.

I started packing, waited for the children to make another pass, told them we were leaving. Even they seemed a little relieved.

My phone began to ring as I pressed the unlock button on my car key. I answered and told Mando to hold on while I stowed the gear and the kids in the car, cranking up the air-conditioning before stepping back out into the expansive, half-empty parking lot so I could speak to him alone. Sweating profusely as the heat radiated off the blacktop, I listened to Mando quietly explain the roller coaster of the day. His sister was gone.

It wasn't until later that night that I found a quiet moment to slow down and absorb the news. Haphazardly stacked dishes filled the sink, and damp beach towels lay piled on the floor in front of the washing machine. There was a tower of mail by the front door and my half-completed puzzle was abandoned on the dining room table. I attended to none of it. The bills and the plates didn't matter. I did; Gina did; my feelings did. I needed that moment to honor her, to honor her life, a life that was so much more than its ending.

I listened to the whirring of the boys' white-noise machines, comforted by their ability to rest. On the couch, my feet tucked up beneath me, I cried for the person our family lost on that day—an aunt, a daughter, a sister. I slowly wiped away tears and whispered to Gina: *I hope you're with your mom.*

29

ARE YOU REMEMBERING TO EAT and drink, Mom?" I asked. Judging by her appearance on FaceTime, sleep was out of the question.

"I'm fine," she insisted. My dad was heading into a second surgery that day to correct the second-most–occluded vessel. The need to be back on the table so quickly underscored the continued severity of his condition.

When Erik died, one of Casey's early posts was about a friend coming over to give her an IV of fluids after she became terribly dehydrated. The worst happens in one person's world, but trains keep running and the sun rises and sets and our bodies still require food and water and clean clothes. Our boring, everyday needs still rudely demand attention.

I finished talking with my parents and then stood to rinse out my tea mug. As I placed it in the dishwasher, I realized I needed to take my own advice and ask myself the basic questions I was asking my mom. My sister-in-law was gone, and my parents were halfway around the world navigating a medical crisis. Life felt dangerously, wildly precarious, so I did the only thing I could: I took care of myself in small, detailed, granular ways.

I swallowed my Zoloft every morning. I took my vitamins. I sipped water from a massive pink water thermos with a matching silicone straw. That evening, I planned to work on a new puzzle. I had therapy with Kim on my schedule. I focused on what I could control, which, as it turned out, was very little.

My dad's second surgery was only partially successful and nothing short of traumatic. My dad wasn't properly sedated and so he lay awake on the table for a nearly seven-hour procedure, watching his soaring heart rate on the monitor to his right. At one point, he remembered hearing the doctor say, in crystal-clear English, "We're in trouble." At another point, my dad's pain was so great that the nurses had to hold him down as he writhed. An American surgeon would later tell us that my dad experienced a heart attack while restrained on that table.

I spoke to my parents the morning after. My dad told me he *knew* his heart couldn't take the stress.

"I just kept thinking, *Please don't let me float away from the table. I don't want to leave*," he told me, and at that point his face crumpled and my mom took the phone, telling me they would call me back. I put my phone down on the counter and sobbed.

Once again, I did all that I could do to take care of myself. I took a shower. I ate breakfast and I swallowed my meds with the water sipped through the pink straw. Allie offered to take the kids to swim practice for me so I could pick up Mando, who was on his way home from Nashville, and I said yes. I remembered to eat. I watched two episodes of *The Good Place*, the only television show I could tolerate, before I went to pick him up.

I was going through the motions, just as Autopilot Julie had done to make it through the spring. But this felt different: these motions were intentional, aimed at carving out space for my feelings, and aimed—at long last—at caring for myself.

When I pulled up to the curb at the Oakland airport Mando was there waiting for me, uncharacteristically pale, nearly washed out by the bright glare of the afternoon sun against the white exterior of the terminal.

I put the car in park and stepped out to hug him. I held him tightly, feeling his fingers grip my waist. As we drove away, we were both quiet.

Mando asked about my dad and I updated him. "He'll be stable enough now to come to the States for any further surgeries. Mom said no more surgeries in Japan." I didn't share all the details or elaborate on the emotions I was feeling. It didn't feel right to give Mando anything else to hold, but I wasn't neglecting myself either—I was grateful to know I'd have my hour of therapy with Kim to process my feelings.

I merged into traffic on the freeway and reached over to squeeze Mando's leg, wanting to be physically connected to him.

"I love you," I said. "I'm glad you're home."

When we walked in the door, the boys were tender with him, caring for their dad in their clumsy, beautiful way.

That night, Mando was asleep as soon as his head hit the

pillow, but I lay awake listening to his heavy, even breaths. I was keyed up, so I began to count my blessings as I tried to quiet my mind, a practice from childhood that I'd recently resurrected. *1. My family, 2. My family, 3. My family.*

And then, mercifully, I was asleep.

30

THE DANCE STEPS OF ANY recovery: two steps forward, one step back. Progress isn't linear. Even though I was charting my path carefully and could point to small markers of progress, missteps were inevitable.

After Mando returned from Nashville, his heart in pieces, I felt a renewed sense of urgency to hurry along my recovery. What if Gina had been able to experience more joy? Could it have helped her avoid the downward spiral? These questions had a galvanizing effect, and I decided I would stop telling everyone—from my family to the mailman—that I *could not possibly* find time for pleasure, for rest, for restoration.

Reclaiming reading as sustenance became a goal. The habit had slid away quietly as each day's minutes were consumed by myriad responsibilities and ill-advised volunteer gigs. And once the anxiety descended, reading for pleasure was impossible. Books required stillness, and I couldn't do stillness for a long stretch of time, couldn't abide the intensity or intimacy of the written word.

But Gina's death took me back to Cathie's advice: Remember what brings you joy. I decided it was time to try again.

I woke early, a regular symptom of my anxious mind and body. I blinked my eyes to let them adjust to the dawn light shining through the shutters of our bedroom. I picked up my Kindle and swiped through the tiny cover thumbnails as I lay in bed, Mando still asleep next to me. I scanned the virtual bookshelf, hundreds of titles staring out at me from the small screen. I paused when I found a book that Amy had recently finished, a book she explicitly said I shouldn't read.

I knew it was risky, but I felt a renewed desire to stop feeling afraid, to toughen up, to hustle along my recovery—and so my finger hovered over *The Woman in the Window* for only a second before I lightly tapped the image to open the book. I was ripping off the Band-Aid, I reasoned.

I angled my body slightly to the side and propped the Kindle up with one hand. Fifteen minutes later, I finished the first chapter in a cold sweat. The main character in the book is an agoraphobic alcoholic who chats online with other agoraphobics, mainly about the ineffectiveness of their medication regimens. There's a suggestion that she may have lost a child, though I'll never know because I stopped after chapter one.

I leaned over and carefully placed my Kindle on my nightstand to pick up my phone to text my sister an SOS: I read the beginning of The Woman in the Window and I'm freaking out.

My phone began to vibrate in my hand less than a minute later. I whispered an abashed greeting as I slipped out of our bedroom and tiptoed down the hall.

"Julie," my sister began, clearly exasperated. "I told you not to read that book!"

"I know," I said. "It was a really bad idea." I laughed awkwardly, my pulse still racing.

I could practically hear her rolling her eyes, but she couldn't help but answer the unspoken question she knew I was asking. "Julie, you're not going to become a person who can't leave the house."

"Okay," I said and exhaled, her words dousing my adrenaline. "So, what you're saying is that reading this book *wasn't* a good idea?"

She laughed with me. We were both experiencing the stress of a father navigating multiple serious surgeries on the other side of the world; my family's love for Mando meant they, too, were grieving his loss, hating his pain. And yet here I was, reading a book I was expressly told not to. Her patience for me was boundless.

"Oh my *gosh*. I will call you later. *Maybe*." I could picture her shaking her head as she pressed the button to disconnect us.

A weird choice and then a moment of lightness with my sister, a person who knew my crazy faults and loved me anyway.

One step back. Maybe.

The boys tumbled out of the car and into the house after swim practice. They bickered briefly about who was on laundry duty, landing on Nolan as the assigned party, as I privately celebrated that they were taking ownership of a job that until recently had been only mine. Nolan placed the swim trunks and towels into the washer as I put away my keys, placed my purse on the bench by the front door, and washed my hands. I smiled a little because I was hungry. It was a good sign. I made three peanut butter and jelly sandwiches and cut up apples, dividing everything onto three white plates.

I watched another episode of *The Good Place* while the boys played on the Wii. I called to check in on Mando, who was working at the office. Unsurprisingly, he'd been quiet since returning from Nashville. I worked on my current puzzle, its rows of bright popsicles arranged in a rainbow spectrum. I inhabited the just-right afternoon, zipping myself into it like a tiny tent that provided momentary shelter from the storm.

I was placing the green puzzle piece into the appropriate popsicle later that evening when I decided to go to a yoga class.

It wasn't picking up a clearly triggering book, but the idea of it still made me nervous. Yoga required states of myself that still felt dangerous: release, stillness, trust, nonjudgmental awareness. I debated whether yoga might feel like "too much" as I sat on the floor, moving on to the turquoise popsicle, sifting through pieces to locate the right colors. Yoga could be a strong step forward or a backward stumble, but I was going to have to take the step at some point. I turned the puzzle pieces around in my hands and found myself suddenly blinking back tears.

Frustration flooded my chest, hot and tight. I didn't want to cry about whether I should go to yoga. I didn't want to feel as if I were making a dangerous, life-changing decision by picking up my phone to search for a nearby class. I despised the excruciating slowness of my progress.

I tried to focus on the fact that there *were* signs of progress. For our sixteenth anniversary a few weeks earlier, Mando had ordered us a Peloton. I'd been angling for one for a while, but because it was so damn expensive, I couldn't justify such a lavish purchase. But he click, click, clicked on the website, was very happy to discover a financing option, and after entering our address, it was confirmed.

We set up the Peloton in the garage, its small footprint allowing us to nestle it into the space between the shelf stocked with spare paper towels and the rack that held the boys' bicycles.

I clipped my cleats into the bike pedals with a satisfying click, remembering my days of road biking in college, thinking back on Ride the Rockies, a weeklong bike tour I'd completed on a tandem with my dad. I tapped the screen to begin my first class.

Just minutes later I felt the first stirrings of panic. As I began to revolve the pedals, I experienced the typical conditions of a body in warm-up—heart pumping, breathing rate increasing, skin itching slightly as the vessels dilated—and my anxiety whispered that this felt dangerous. I did my best to ignore the whispers and stay focused on the instructor's cues, increasing the resistance slightly as the tears filled my eyes and my body slightly shook.

For twenty minutes, I clung to every motivational phrase uttered by the instructor, Jen Sherman, and tried to absorb the energy from every one of her wide smiles. I cried again in relief when the class ended, propping my arms on the handlebars and setting my head in my hands. Every day after that one, I climbed on the bike, and nearly every day I cried. I was so tired of my fragility, my anxious thoughts, and the way I second-guessed nearly everything. But I kept getting back on the bike, telling myself that it was something.

I brought up the second-guessing with Kim, sharing my frustration with yet another pattern that felt difficult to change. Agonizing predecision *and* postdecision made me feel defeated. I couldn't seem to help myself. I brought up the Zoloft as an example. Although it was clear that the medication was necessary and working well for me, I would still ask myself if I really *needed* it. "Why am I doing all this back and forth, even about decisions I've already made?" I asked her, frustrated.

"You skipped over the key point there," Kim answered. "You already made the decision. You considered the options and then you made a choice. You're capable of doing that." The agonizing was optional, she suggested, but it had become an entrenched pattern. It was something to notice. Paying attention had become step one in nearly every situation.

As I pulled up the app on my phone and typed *yoga* into the search bar, I knew, deep down, that I'd already made the decision, just as I made the decision to get on the Peloton every day, just as I made the decision to swallow the Zoloft every morning. Maybe Kim was right and I could spare myself the relentless doubt.

I chose a brand-new studio, its anonymity feeling safe; if I needed to leave midway through the class, I could comfort myself with the knowledge I probably wouldn't see those people again (as if yogis would ever be considered a highly judgmental group). Quickly, before doubt could raise another objection, I typed in my memorized credit card number and hit purchase, committing to a class the following evening. My phone pinged and I was greeted with the message that I was confirmed for class. The confirmation email came with an enthusiastic smiley-face emoji at the bottom that I eyed suspiciously. Didn't that rosy-cheeked face know I was a hot mess?

The next day, I summoned my courage and went. I found a place in the back of the room and rolled out my purple yoga mat, smoothing the edges down. I sat quietly with my eyes closed until the class began, and then, for an hour and fifteen minutes, I practiced and sweated and moved my miraculous body. When it was time for Savasana at the end of the class, I lay down on my back and released my limbs into the floor. I let grateful tears drip out of the corners of my eyes and trail down the sides of my hot, sweaty face, felt some of them collecting in the shallow whorls of my ears. I was taking another step by reconnecting to my body— to its strength, to my strength.

It was quiet. I found momentary respite from my world, from its loss and need and upheaval. It was just me, there with myself, the part of me that exists outside of my disparate pieces and roles and obligations and imagined obligations.

I'm enough, I thought. *And I'm okay*.

One step forward.

31

As the summer opened up before us, my dad returned to the Tokyo apartment to heal and rest. Though the surgeries had technically been successful, he continued to say that something didn't feel quite right. He couldn't put a finer point on it than to express this general knowing, but his unease persisted. My mom managed (and occasionally micromanaged) his recovery as she prepared for Dad to have his final procedure at Stanford. Thousands of miles away from their high-rise home, I continued to see tiny signs of growth and movement back toward a self I recognized. Mando, on the other hand, sank into a mild depression as he began to grieve the loss of Gina.

Depression is an ill-fitting garment that looks different on everyone. On me, it looked anxious and flighty, a feeling of being trapped inside my own head. Mando's sadness manifested itself physically. He had stomach issues and random pains. He had a persistent sinus infection and pink eye that was stubbornly resistant to antibiotics. He slept horribly and was exhausted and often short-tempered. It didn't help that Gina's service was delayed until late July, nearly six weeks away. Mando's body was storing that impossible grief, unable to release the pain of her loss.

I managed our social lives around how Mando was doing. I canceled plans at the last minute or attended necessary events alone, while still maintaining a careful watch on my own energy levels.

In the midst of dealing with Gina's death and my father's health scare, I hadn't been focused on whether the library job would be too much in the fall. To have a break from this rumination felt nearly blissful. The events requiring my attention and freeing me from this preoccupation were themselves draining and objectively awful, but I felt more in the now, less in the future. I was grateful for Kim's support as I implemented small changes and felt the resultant shifts in my inner life.

I walked into the house one afternoon after having called Cathie from the backyard. We had made dinner plans for the two families, and though we were meeting up in only a few hours, I called to tell her Mando didn't have the energy for it. He was too sad, and too empty, and I was supremely thankful for the grace of friends who understood his (and our) limits. I wiped away quick tears of gratitude before opening the sliding glass door to go back inside.

"Did you call her?" Mando asked from the couch as I came into the room.

"Yes, and they totally understood. Zero issue there." I slid the door closed behind me and went to plug in my phone.

"Thank you, Julie," he said. "I'm sorry."

"Love, it's all good. Please don't apologize. You know that I get it. I mean, we both remember Memorial Day." I plopped down on the couch next to him and squeezed his shoulder.

Mando paused for a beat before he looked at me and said, "I'm sorry, Julie. I couldn't fully understand where you were on that day, and now I do."

And to this day, I mark that moment as one of the most loving of our marriage. His simple utterance made me feel seen and solid, and the memory of that shitty day at the country club never stung again.

32

I SAT ON KIM'S COUCH on a Wednesday in the middle of July. Her room was cool, a welcome reprieve from the punishing heat outside.

"I had a bad day yesterday," I told her. "I felt low."

"What happened?"

"Well, Mando's tired—he's still not sleeping well—and his pink eye came back, even though he's already treated it once. He's distant, which I obviously understand, but I feel lonely. And I made the program for Gina's service yesterday, so that didn't help anything."

The previous afternoon, I had used my limited Photoshop skills to resize photos of Gina and position them with graphics of watercolor yellow roses. There were snapshots, an engagement photo, a wedding shot. I scanned in photos of Gina and Mando as children in a department store, the two of them seated on a small riser covered in brown carpet, their bright smiles, haircuts, and Mando's polyester pants serving as an early-1980s date stamp.

I looked at Gina's beautiful brown eyes and imagined Becky standing behind the photographer, beaming with pride at her two children.

I could avoid reading thrillers and filter my Instagram, but I wanted to design the program for her service, to perform that small, intentional act of love, even though I knew it would be hard.

I sat and stared at those photos as I sized and arranged, as I layered and shifted the images to fit onto the program, a small double-sided card with the dates of her birth and death. The boys rode their bikes outside, and I sat alone in the house, repositioning text, making small adjustments, undoing changes. And then, after forty-five minutes, I let out a huge sob and put my head in my hands. I sat at the desk and cried for the stupid, horrible loss of her.

"We booked our plane tickets to Colorado for the memorial service," I told Kim. I knew it would be an emotionally raw weekend for us, but I also hoped that it would bring Mando some closure.

"You're handling a lot right now," Kim said. "I'm not surprised you're feeling sad."

These basic affirmations from Kim were invaluable. It was reassuring to hear her observations that my plate was indeed full, that hard things were justifiably hard, that what I was feeling or experiencing was normal. I'd done years of unappreciated work, and the person who appreciated my efforts least had been me. Kim was training me to see this invisible load, to count it as valid and worthy of attention and accommodation. She reminded me that it was normal to have bad days and normal to be an emotional, feeling person in a fucked-up world. Feelings weren't an early warning sign I was an unbalanced nut. I was merely responding to the ups and downs of life.

"How was Vegas?" I asked her, changing the subject. Kim had taken one of her daughters to Sin City for a dance competition over the Fourth of July. "Was it the temperature of the sun?"

"Pretty much," she said, laughing, "but she's graduating from high school soon, so that's the last one we'll do together."

"Are you ready to be an empty-nester?" I occasionally asked Kim these types of questions, inquiring about her life. This professional therapeutic relationship developed naturally in our visits and was tremendously comforting, like a friendship, but with tight, clearly articulated boundaries and payment with my American Express.

"It'll be an adjustment," she responded neutrally, "but it's the right time." She paused, creating conversational space for me to shift the direction back to, well, me.

Therapy provided me the luxury of an hour of unashamed self-centeredness. Every week I had sixty minutes with a wise, nonjudgmental professional, and I could use that time to ramble or rant or rage. It was cathartic for a woman who often tied her self-worth to her ability to hear and respond to the needs of others. Putting voice to my inner experience was good medicine.

"Nolan's starting middle school this fall," I said, presenting the next topic, "and it's weird to think that he'll go to college someday."

"That transition to middle school is a big one. How's he feeling about it?"

"Oh, he's totally ready. He's going to do well." I knew this to be true. "But in the bigger picture, he's closer to leaving home. It feels like the beginning of the part where he walks into his own life." I paused, trying to pin down the source of my emotion. "I don't want things to change."

"But *everything* changes," Kim said gently. "And thank God it does, right?"

My automatic, knee-jerk thought was, *Are we sure about that, Kim? Because if things change, then who knows what will happen? It could all really go tits up.* But I knew she was trying to help me see change differently, to break my pattern of predicting the worst. Kim was helping me not to try on every tragic story or medical malady I encountered like a pair of leather pants that had no hope of getting past my knees. She was trying to help me believe that perhaps the future held joy and wonder in addition to the inevitable pain.

"I know you're right," I said with a sigh. "I think about when the boys were small, and I like life better now. I just want them to be happy in the future. I want them to have happy lives, and the world is such an insane place."

"You can't control the future, Julie. But it sounds like you're doing the best you can to provide them with tools to help them choose lives that will bring them joy."

"I guess if this summer has taught me anything it would be that I can't control a damn thing," I said to Kim, thinking of Gina, my dad, Mando's sadness. "I know that's true. But I want to get it right."

"Get *what* right?"

"Life, I guess." I shrugged, but we both knew I craved the impossible. I wanted desperately to believe that the right choices would insulate me from pain. But at the same time, I knew that nothing could protect me from the harsh reality of the world: shit happens, all the time, even to the best people, the most loved people. Beautiful lives can be smashed to smithereens in a thousand ways.

Kim waited.

"I don't want to be afraid anymore," I told her. "Like feeling low yesterday. I want to chalk that up to a bad day without worrying that I'm backsliding, that it's a bad sign."

"You're able to articulate what's happening," Kim said, "and when you first started therapy you were carried away by that fear without understanding it. Now you can name it."

"That's true. I guess that's a sign I'm getting stronger." Maybe I wasn't helpless. Maybe I wouldn't feel afraid forever.

Kim put it simply. "You *are* getting stronger." Kim agreed with Mister Rogers, the television companion of my childhood: what's mentionable is manageable.

I left Kim's office and took the boys for a Slurpee. When I got home, I worked on my puzzle for a while until Mando came home. *Yesterday was a bad day*, I thought to myself, carefully placing the pieces. *And that's okay.*

I'd promised the boys I'd take them to the pool that afternoon. As they put on swim trunks and bitched good-naturedly about sunscreen, I took a moment to choose a book for myself. I walked the length of my bookshelf, skimming the spines with my hand as I considered the titles. A reread of a gentle, beautiful book felt manageable.

While the boys swam and flopped in the water with the friends they'd found at the pool, I stretched out in the plastic lounge chair on my striped towel and luxuriated in the sunshine, the freedom, the vitamin D. Naturally, my next thought was about skin cancer, but I told myself *no,* using firm self-talk with my rebellious toddler mind. I reached into the large swim bag and pushed aside the sunscreen and snacks to pull out *Gift from the Sea,* a book given to me by my mom when Nolan was young. She mailed it not long after Nolan's first birthday and wrote in the card in her distinct cursive: "I first read this book when you were young. I've read it often over the years, and there has always been something for me in its pages."

I ran my hand over the roughly textured light turquoise cover, opening the book to read the words that Anne Morrow Lindbergh wrote in 1955:

> To be a woman is to have interests and duties raying out in all directions from the central mother-core, like spokes from the hub of a wheel. The pattern of our lives is essentially circular. We must be open to all points of the compass; husband, children, friends, home, community; stretched out, exposed, sensitive like a spider's web to each breeze that blows, to each call that comes. How difficult for us, then, to achieve a balance in the midst of these contradictory tensions, and yet how necessary for the proper functioning of our lives.

I dog-eared the page, the sunscreen from my fingers leaving light grease spots next to the folded triangle of paper. These words had been written seven decades earlier, and yet they spoke directly to me, allowing me to experience a certain magical connection that can be found only in a book.

I looked up at the boys laughing in the sun, the skin of their backs a deep brown from daily swim team practice. I watched them push friends into the pool, watched them dive in next, only to emerge from beneath the surface of the sparkling water with wide smiles. I observed them in all their fumbling, perfect awkwardness, all limbs and laughter. They were enough, just as they were.

How funny that Lindbergh's wheel imagery for a balanced, strong life mirrored the one Tim had chosen during my initial visit with him in the spring. A wheel functions best when it's balanced, centered. That was the work I was doing that summer. I was learning to make space for rest. I was learning, slowly, to attend first to my center.

What if I gazed at myself as I gazed at my kids, who were glorious in their perfect bodies, with the small curls at their hairline and their angular elbows and their still-crooked teeth? What if I could accept my own imperfections as I accepted theirs? What if I told myself, every day, that I was enough?

I rolled over to my back, closing my eyes and tipping my face up to the sun. In this moment of stillness, my mind stayed focused on this image of a wheel. Talking to Kim, shedding worries and obligations and the dreaded shoulds—I was strengthening my wheel, reinforcing the spokes, painting the center a brighter color that would be more visible to others. I was repairing, but I was also remaking, making sure the wheel was stronger and more resilient. I was laboring to create a newer version that would adapt more effectively to changes in terrain and weather.

Lying there by the pool, basking in the sun and the joy of my children and a moment of rest, I wasn't achieving or striving or working. And somehow, miraculously, I was proud of myself. I was enough.

33

WE SAID GOODBYE TO GINA on a bluebird day in Colorado. We scattered her ashes near her mom's, in a place we imagined Gina would've liked. There's much and little to say about a heavy day like that one, but what remains with me are the acts of love that pierced the fog of grief that weekend: a text from Kim, calls from my family, hugs from friends who'd traveled to be there at Mando's side. When I saw the tidy stack of clean, folded towels waiting for us in the guest bathroom of our friends' home, I felt so perfectly cared for that I wanted to weep.

As we sat on our friends' deck after the service, the boys playing on the grass nearby and the sun setting against the mountains, I could feel Mando unknotting, could see the slight opening of his chest as his shoulders pulled back and down into their proper position. Colorado was home to us. And now, in a way, his sister was home too.

But the weekend had depleted his emotional reserves, and by the time we arrived at the airport on Sunday morning, he was miles past empty. I was exhausted. The boys were tired. We were relieved and felt grateful that Gina's service had honored her, but we were wrung out, impatient, and suffering from a major emotional hangover.

Nolan nearly got trapped in the doors of the airport train when Mando jumped on ahead of us, not leaving sufficient time for the rest of us to board before the train's departure. With so much solo work travel, Mando was accustomed to moving at his own speed.

"Nolan, pay attention!" Mando hissed as Nolan rubbed his shoulder where it hit the train door. I glared at Mando as the train picked up speed, moving us through the tunnel to the next stop.

After we arrived in the terminal, Eli failed to maneuver his suitcase onto the escalator in a timely manner, causing a quick stumble that incited another sharp reprimand from Mando. "Eli, what are you doing?" His voice was loud, and Eli fought tears of embarrassment and frustration.

"Hey," I said in a sharp, warning voice. Mando stood a few steps above me on the escalator, and he turned around. "Get a grip," I said, delivering my command louder than was strictly necessary. He gave me a hard look before turning to face forward, then walked a few steps ahead of us to the gate.

We had become the family publicly losing their shit. We marched to the gate, dark clouds over our heads.

We found an abandoned group of chairs away from innocent bystanders, and the boys sat down. I kneeled before them and said, "Guys, we're all a mess and it's okay. This was a hard weekend." I spoke the words that I imagined Kim would speak to me, to all of us, this hot dumpster fire of a family in the C terminal.

I looked up at Mando, who was digging through his backpack for his water. I said his name and he looked up. In his face, I saw only weariness. I stood next to him, grabbed his hand, and said, "We just need to get home." We hugged each other and I squeezed him hard, because sometimes words are stubborn and useless.

I told the boys that their dad and I would go grab snacks, removing Mando from them because I understood his stress. He was trying to deal with his family when what he really needed was to care for himself.

Mando and I walked through the terminal, and I felt him squeeze my hand, a quiet gesture of thanks. We moved through the masses of people and the competing airport sounds, and as we stood in the line to purchase overpriced burgers and fries and fountain Cokes, I felt the stirrings of hope. We took a grease-stained bag from the counter when our number was called, and we walked slowly back to our children, feeling the frustration and love and forgiveness that make up the resilient bonds of a family.

34

THE BACKPACKS SAT IN THE foyer next to sneakers and water bottles, all of it as bright and unblemished as a new box of crayons. The boys' outfits were laid out neatly in their rooms. Schedules were printed and memorized, carpools arranged, haircuts fresh. We were ready for the first day of school.

I did all my tasks slowly, methodically, as if moving carefully through my morning would be a ritual to ensure luck for the year. Mando was working from home and prepared breakfast for me while I showered, blow-dried my hair, and swiped my lashes with mascara. I walked out into the kitchen and saw the boys were already perched on their stools at the counter. I said goodbye, and Mando gave me a hug; the boys wished me luck and kissed me on the cheek.

Mando had prepared breakfast burritos that could be frozen for an upcoming morning—he was now on weekday breakfast duty when he wasn't traveling. The night before, laundry had been dumped on the couch and the boys had come to claim their own items, to place them not-so-carefully in their drawers. I was caring for only myself that morning, and Mando would be ensuring that the boys got to school on time. He snapped the first-day-of-school picture. This time I was in it too.

Throughout the summer, I'd deferred thinking about the library but had nurtured the hope that if I understood myself a bit better, the job could be part of who I was becoming instead of a roadblock to my mental and physical health. Now it was time to test that hope.

I walked into the garage and placed my purse into the basket on my bicycle, taking a moment to be still. I took a deep breath to reassure my mind and body that all was well. I checked to make sure I had all my items for the morning: water bottle, school keys, cell phone, extra allergy meds that had earned a permanent place in my purse after I accepted that the presence of the little pink pills offered valuable reassurance.

I rolled down the driveway and across the cul-de-sac, turning onto the paved path that would usher me to the school. The early light filtered through the still-green leaves of the trees, illuminating a tiny line just above the grass where the dew was evaporating. It was a beautiful morning.

The week before, I shared my last-minute end-of-summer fears and hopes with Cathie. "Julie, if it's too much, you'll know, but you should try," she said, reiterating her message from months earlier. "You've made a lot of changes over the summer."

The changes I had made were small but impactful. I asked for help slightly more often, and I said no far more often. I embraced rest and put some items on my to-do list purely because they brought me joy.

"I know you're right," I told her. "Plus, I need to try out my new work motto."

"What's that?" Cathie asked.

"Be Adequate."

She laughed, and then I started to laugh too, even though I wasn't joking. Be Adequate was my new guiding principle. Perfection was something to let go of, not something to strive for.

"I think you can do this," Cathie said. I was finally beginning to believe that she was right.

I exchanged postsummer pleasantries with the office staff before passing through to the library. I sat down at my desk to boot up my computer. As I waited for it to whir to life, I thought about writing "Be Adequate" on a Post-it Note, but it felt strangely personal, like an inside joke that would require too much explanation. Instead, I chose three pieces of advice from Zen master Thich Nhat Hanh: Smile. Breathe. Go Slowly. I wrote the three short directives on the small yellow square using block print with a black Sharpie and stuck it on the short counter next to my keyboard, resolving to look at it every time feelings of anxiety crept in.

What a difference, to expect that I'd feel unsettled at times— and to prepare accordingly, to create an opportunity for grace instead of judgment. I knew there would be waves ahead, but I was no longer afraid of drowning.

And the day was, by all accounts, a success. The only snag

wasn't revealed until later, when Nolan came home from his first day of middle school and said, "*Mom*. Everyone else was prepared! They all had notebooks and stuff!" He didn't seem upset so much as shocked. He told me he had to borrow a pencil from a friend.

"Wait, what?" I had grown accustomed to our elementary model. I donated fifty bucks per child and all supplies were purchased, ready and waiting, uniformly arranged in their miniature desks. All I had to do was send the kids on the first day with a backpack, a lunch, and, of course, a water bottle. (These kids are seemingly unable to go for ten consecutive minutes without water, though the only memories I have of drinking water as a child are when I got it out of someone's hose.)

When Nolan described watching all his friends pull the necessary items out of their backpacks while his was completely empty, the loveliest thing happened: we laughed. I laughed so hard I cried, picturing my poor type A child feeling sweaty and unprepared.

I scrounged up a notebook and ripped the used pages from the front before presenting it to Nolan. Mando took him shopping the next day, and I didn't feel flustered or guilty or like I had somehow failed.

First day of school: adequate and, somehow, perfect.

35

A FEW WEEKS INTO THE school year, I faced up to one of my fears. I took a deep, quivering breath as I waited for the medical assistant to return with the syringe containing the tetanus booster. I had made significant progress, but shots were still a massive trigger for me. My sweaty hands rubbed against the crinkly paper on the table before I set them in my lap, using my new tools to ground myself: breathing, self-talk, allowing the fear to be acknowledged and present. *You can do this,* I told myself.

I'd told Mando in the morning that I was getting an injection later that day, asking him unabashedly if he could come with me.

I had a holiday off from school, but he was in the midst of a stressful morning, dealing with a badly behaved spreadsheet and a string of problems that were wholly out of his control. He kept his eyes on his laptop as he responded, "I have a call at that time. I need to take care of this mess."

Just an hour earlier, I had made the appointment assuming he'd be available. I'd called at the last minute on purpose, wanting a quick window of time between planning and execution. The less time I had to overthink, the better.

"I'm sorry," he said casually, not understanding that this was a big deal for me, a major hurdle I was trying to clamber over.

I stood next to Mando as he typed, waiting for him to change his mind, waiting for him to realize that I was, for one of the first times in our marriage, asking him to do something with me because I was frightened. I wasn't explaining away or ignoring my need but stating it: "I'm afraid. Will you come with me?"

But just as progress wasn't linear in my personal recovery, neither was it linear in our relationship. He knew I'd handle it because I always managed to handle it—whatever *it* was. And in that moment, his strengths—his ability to compartmentalize, his responsibility and drive, his focus—became his weaknesses. I stalked out of the room, too incensed to care that he was (just) trying to do his job on a stressful workday.

I drove to the doctor's office, distracting myself with an audiobook. I walked into the small room and mentally reviewed the lifetime of uneventful injections I'd received (all, minus the one that had been specifically designed to affect me). And then I took deep breaths as I signed the consent form. I waited for the nurse to return, closing my eyes and exhaling the very mantra I'd used on The Night I Couldn't Turn Off the Lights. *You're okay, Julie. You can do this.* I felt my heart pound against my rib cage. *You can do this. You're okay.*

And this time, the mantra was enough. The nurse returned with the predrawn syringe, and I continued to breathe deeply as she performed the injection. A moment, a pinch, another moment, and mercifully, it was done. The anger I felt at Mando's response didn't diminish the sense of victory I experienced as the nurse put a small Band-Aid on my shoulder. I'd survived the fear and had received my first injection since that day in November. And this time, with a pinprick of the needle, I was a tiny bit stronger.

That night, sitting across the couch from Mando after the kids had gone to bed, I was able to communicate how I felt about the morning. I'd told him I needed him, but he hadn't responded to that need.

Mando and I had both softened over the summer, and it didn't take much for him to understand and apologize. "I felt bad as soon as you left for the appointment," he said.

"Sometimes I need you, even though it's irrational and immediate," I said. "I don't want to feel like that's an inconvenience for you." Just months ago, I wouldn't have allowed myself to be so vulnerable, even with my husband.

"You're never an inconvenience," he said. "I'm sorry. I won't do it that way again."

It felt remarkably freeing to be able to talk like this, to have a new level of connectedness and openness between us after so many years of marriage. Mistakes happen. Wrong moves happen. But that night, as we cozied up to watch *Real Housewives of Beverly Hills*, I knew we could recover when they did. Resilience and forgiveness tasted much sweeter than perfection.

To the casual listener, it might have seemed as though I wasted no time before tattling on Mando during my session with Kim the next day.

"I'm proud of myself for getting through the shot on my own, but what wasn't good is that I asked Mando to come with me and he didn't," I said. "He would've had to change a scheduled call, but I never ask him to take care of me like this. I said clearly that I needed him, and he didn't respond to that. So I was upset."

"Of course you were," Kim said. "Did you talk about it after the fact?"

"Yeah, we talked it through last night." Kim knew by then that I loved a thorough argument autopsy, and I walked her through what we'd both said.

"I'm proud of you for expressing your needs."

I was too—and I was proud of the way we'd found resolution. The evening's conversation with Mando was another tiny miracle. "It's like we're relearning each other in some ways," I told Kim. "Today when I was driving here, I was thinking about how he and I are going to keep changing as individuals, so we'll have to keep learning each other, and every time we change, the relationship will change. We'll have to keep doing this *forever*." I said it melodramatically, but Kim only smiled and nodded.

"Yes, I think that's true," she responded.

"Sounds tiring," I said, and we laughed. It was a preposterous ask that intimacy, the bedrock of our best relationships, would require so much work.

36

ALTHOUGH THE START TO THE school year had felt okay and sometimes even reached the threshold of good, Back to School Night arrived on a day when I was exhausted. I'd finished up at the library and done a quick turnaround to carpool the boys and their assorted teammates to practice, Mando was out of town, and the events at each school were simultaneous. I couldn't be in two places at once. There was no perfect solution—something that would've put me on edge the year before.

I considered attending Eli's, but I was more familiar with what was happening in his classroom since I worked down the hall and already knew the teacher well. I texted her to see if I'd miss anything there. I saw the three dots appear and then her reply popped up: No, it's all good.

Nolan sat at the counter, eating an orange. "Hey," I said. "Do you know what they're covering tonight at the middle school?"

"No," he said, unhelpfully. "I have a schedule for you of all my classes, but I don't think you have to go."

I didn't *have* to go. His response presented me with a new possibility. Maybe I wouldn't attend either event. Maybe I could just have a quiet night at home with the boys to recharge after a long day. I had friends going. I could check in with them to see if I'd missed anything important. Teachers would email regarding anything critical.

I paused, entertaining the idea. I worked with Kim over the summer to hear my own voice, and that evening, I did: skipping would be fine. "Is there anything I'll miss?" I asked Nolan.

He was putting his dish in the dishwasher and rinsing his hands at the sink. "We made this quiz for our parents."

I felt a little stab of guilt, but I pushed it firmly aside. "Could you bring the quiz home, do you think? Because I do want to see that."

"Sure," he said with a shrug.

"Nolan," I said, and he turned to me. "Will you be disappointed if I don't go?"

"Mom, I don't care. I don't think you'll miss anything." He walked away to start his homework, a moment in which he was his father's son: practical and straightforward.

I checked in with Eli in the same manner, and his response mirrored Nolan's.

Nobody minded that I was choosing to be adequate, that I was opting for the easier night. I didn't want to sit through two hours of presentations about class rules and expectations at either school. I was already familiar with what would be covered, and I knew what the boys were working on academically. Tonight, I could take advantage of the fact that I was up to speed and let myself coast a little.

No one was giving out gold stars for attendance, and even if they were, I didn't want or need one. Finally.

Relieved and proud of myself, I took the boys to pick up burgers from In-N-Out and we watched *Teen Titans Go!* while we dipped our fries in ketchup and sipped our milkshakes. It was a perfect night.

When I put the boys to bed, I thanked them. I told them I was learning how to do less and that they helped me accomplish that. Before giving Nolan a kiss, I told him, "You know, the other part is that I really like being with you, and I'm happy I got to do that tonight." His head was burrowed into his pillow, but he lifted it to give me a kiss. He mumbled, "Love you," as I closed his door.

I turned off the hallway light as I turned into Eli's room. I rubbed lotion on his feet, and then, as I tucked the covers tightly around him, I spoke the same words to him. He smiled at me and told me he loved me, extricating his bony little arms from the cocoon of blankets to give me a tight hug.

I'm enough for them. This thought glowed warmly inside me, dispelling any remaining shadows of guilt. *I'm enough because I'm me, and I'm enough because I'm theirs.*

The feeling was better than any gold star I'd ever received.

37

ONE OF MY FAVORITE MEMORIES of my dad took place moments before Eli was born.

My mom and Mando had left the room for a moment, and I was waiting to be wheeled back for my scheduled C-section with Eli. It was just my dad and me. I picked idly at the tape covering my just-inserted IV. "I'm not sure if having a second baby was such a good idea," I said, only half joking.

He widened his eyes and let out a quick snort of laughter. Then he put his hand over mine. "Well, Julie, I think that horse is out of the barn."

I gave an unsure smile.

"It's going to be good," he said, and just like that, I believed him. I relaxed into his reassurance and put my head back on the pillow, laughing a little at my own absurdity.

As it turned out, he was right. Nolan may have stabbed himself in the eye with a fork later that day at Red Robin, but Eli's appearance in the world gave our family the balance it needed. It was more than good.

My dad's initial heart diagnosis had identified three blocked vessels. When he had recovered from his two procedures in Japan addressing the LAD and the second-most-occluded vessel, he was cleared for travel to California. His scans were sent ahead to Stanford so that a surgeon named Dr. Aden could prepare to place the stent in the final occluded vessel.

After a plane trip and a week of preop evaluations and appointments, my dad was again the one awaiting surgery, the one in need of reassurance. He and my mom were both feeling traumatized and justifiably frightened after his harrowing experiences in Japan, and now he was about to go through the same procedure for a third time so that doctors could prop open the last vessel like a broken garage door with a spent spring that would no longer bear its weight. As I drove south to Palo Alto, the location of Stanford Hospital, my hope was to provide the same support for them that they'd so regularly provided for me as I grew up.

Amy had flown in from Austin for the surgery, and while the admitting staff snapped the requisite hospital bracelet around my dad's wrist, she and I staked out a small, protected alcove in the waiting room. When my parents joined us, both looking nervous and edgy, I did my best to distract them by being ridiculous. "I hope the surgeon didn't party too hard last night," I joked.

My mom rolled her eyes and my dad laughed, but I knew he was well beyond anxious. It was the distant look in the eyes that gave it away.

I spent the next five minutes pretending to be a surgeon with a vicious hangover, complete with a wide variety of muffled gag noises and references to the sweats and the shakes. "Nurse, could you maybe bring that emesis basin a little closer?" I said, standing up and leaning over to put my hands on my knees like I was going to heave before shooting out my hand to say, "Scalpel," in a strangled, pained voice.

My mom laughed but shook her head. My sister egged me on. But my dad laughed so hard he cried, which was, of course, my goal. He was still laughing when the nurse came to take him back to prep for the procedure, my mom getting up to follow him and shooting my sister and me a mildly concerned look that suggested she wasn't sure whether she could trust us to watch her purse.

She returned about twenty minutes later and told us to go back and see him, looking as strong as I'd ever seen her.

Amy and I went back one at a time to give words of love and encouragement. The time for cheap laughs had passed. My dad cried, and I cried, but I told him the same words he told me when I was the one lying in the hospital bed.

"It's going to be good, Dad."

Thankfully, it was.

The surgery was successful and proper sedation really made things a lot easier. After my mom visited my dad in recovery, I took her place so she and Amy could pick up prescriptions at the pharmacy. The nurse gave me a few guidelines before she drifted away to monitor the other occupants of the long, quiet room. The soft beeps and chirps punctuated the hushed murmurs that gently echoed through the thin curtains. Dad had to lie flat with his hands at his sides for the first stretch of time, and so I gave him tiny sips of water through a straw. He asked me how the procedure went.

"It went well, Dad. You were right. Dr. Tanaka made a mistake, but Dr. Aden fixed it."

"I knew it," he mumbled, his speech still slow from the anesthesia. "Remember, I told you? I said something wasn't right after that second procedure."

He closed his eyes and drifted in and out of sleep, and then, ten minutes later, he asked me again how the procedure went. We had a variation of the same conversation.

"I knew something was wrong." He landed on this point again, emphatically. Even in postanesthetic fog, he seemed relieved to have his suspicions confirmed, his fears validated.

The nurse returned about twenty minutes later and told my dad he could be angled up just slightly and have some juice. Another twenty minutes passed before I noticed the color slowly returning to his cheeks, although he wasn't allowed to lift his arms yet.

"Tell me again how the procedure went," he said. The fog was clearing, and I knew he'd retain more details this time.

I fed him a bowl of oatmeal, placing small amounts onto the spoon before delivering them to his mouth. He carefully chewed the tiny grains of each bite.

When he finished, I set the empty bowl aside and gave him a sip of water. I smiled at him, grateful that he was alive, that he was there, physically next to me instead of halfway around the world, and that he had my mom as a partner and advocate. I set the water down on the rolling table beside the bed. When my dad closed his eyes for a moment, I pulled my phone out of my pocket. I'd been texting Mando updates all day, and now I sent him a quick message to tell him I'd leave soon in order to beat the worst of the inevitable northbound afternoon traffic.

Until then, I was content to sit there with my dad.

38

Nearly every year since we were married, Mando has gone on a fall trip with a small group of childhood and college friends. The planning phase lasts for months: accommodations, meals, tee times, who's bringing the Coors Light. The trip was tradition, part of the rhythm of our years—as well as an annual source of contention.

It always began well. I would wish him a good trip and a fun time with his friends, and I would mean it. But as the weekend progressed, I'd feel a mounting resentment. Why should he get to have all the fun? Why was I always left with the home and child-care responsibilities? Why did it feel like a big deal for me to carve out time to go to yoga for an hour and he seemed to have no problem skipping out for multiple days? Why was I the only one who felt pressure to be endlessly present and available for the boys? Couldn't he see the imbalance?

By day three, the unraveling would be complete, and we'd be bickering on the phone and via text. I once sent him a message that said only **Night** and then turned off my phone until the next day. By the time he walked back through the door, guys' trip was officially Fucking Guys' Trip.

"But this year is different," I told Kim. "I *want* him to go and find that rest, to be able to goof around with his friends and make jokes and drink a little too much beer. I want that for him. It's made me think about why the trip has been a trigger for me in the past."

"Do you have an answer for that?"

"Well . . ." I paused for dramatic effect. "I know this is really going to surprise you, but it's a variation on the same theme." Kim laughed lightly at my sarcasm. "I withheld care from myself. If I told Mando I was going on a girls' weekend, he would support it 100 percent. He's never bothered when I leave, and he encourages it. But I never do. I shut myself down before even asking for his support. I always have a ready reason why it would be more tricky or difficult for me to go."

In fairness, it did seem to be legitimately harder for the moms I knew to get away. When my friends left their husbands in charge, they typically handed them typed instructions for the day and maybe left a meal in the fridge. There was extra work involved in taking a day off (or two, if a mom got supremely lucky). When Mando went on his guys' trip, he simply packed his bag and went. During the trip, he had the extra gift of peace of mind that everything was running fine at home. He took that peace of mind for granted, and I resented him for it.

"I need to get over this idea that I can never check out," I told Kim. "I'm already making small steps toward it by leaving and doing things just for me. And Mando and the boys are super sweet about it—they encourage it."

Even though I'd occasionally painted them as insatiable leeches, the people who loved me wanted me to take time for myself. They wanted me to balance my needs with theirs, to be well and whole. I was allowed to hand off responsibilities to my husband, my kids, and others, and I was even allowed to phone it in if that's what was best for my overall balance and wellness.

"I know I'm hard on myself," I admitted to Kim. "And I think I've been hard on Mando."

"How do you mean?"

"Well, because I'm always trying to prove myself, to reassure myself that I'm doing enough, I've sometimes put that on him too. I've resented Mando's ability to take time for himself. And deep down I think I also wanted Mando to prove that I was the most important person in his life by not going. I wanted him to prove that our family was his priority."

"But obviously you're the most important person in his life, and he seems very committed to the boys and your family."

"Right. And why wouldn't I trust that? Why the constant need for proof?" I shook my head. I had a beautiful life and a strong marriage. It was as if I built a house and it was standing—I even knew I built it well—but I spent most of the day obsessively checking my work instead of *living* in the house, instead of enjoying the relationships that existed and breathed inside its walls.

It was true that houses sometimes got termites. Relationships between flawed, changing humans could go wildly off course. It's impossible to fully discern what the future will hold. But if I spent all my time preparing for the worst possibility, anxiously watching for signs that the house was crumbling, I was in danger of creating a self-fulfilling prophecy. Doubt would spread through the timbers and the joists, weakening the wood as effectively as any infestation.

Therapy with Kim helped me rewrite some of the stories I had grown accustomed to telling myself. She taught me that worrying didn't necessarily make the future brighter, but it did make the present darker. And she reminded me—again and again, as many times as I needed it—that I was strong enough to handle whatever happened. She helped me see that my strength wasn't rooted in my ability to do it all seamlessly and perfectly; it was rooted in the fact that I'd never abandon myself again.

I was learning to ask myself the question I'd ask someone I love: *What do you need?* And then whatever answer arrived—be still, exercise, meditate, lie on the couch with a book, text Kim some depressed-looking bitmojis and ask if she has appointments available—I did it.

That day, I left Kim's office and walked down the stairs, pushing open the door into the cloudy early evening. I decided I'd get a coffee before heading home and zipped up my jacket against the sharp breeze.

This tiny freedom was one I wouldn't have granted myself in the spring. I was now consciously taking a moment to absorb the hour I'd just spent with Kim like a therapeutic version of a yoga Savasana. The girl behind the counter called my name, and I approached to take my flat white from her hands, thanking her.

I sat down at a table by the window, putting my hands around the paper cup to feel the warmth seep into my cold fingers.

The first few weeks of school were a new dance for our family, and though we'd been stepping on one another's toes on and off, we were finding a new rhythm as I relinquished some of the responsibilities that never should've been solely mine. The boys made their own lunches. We cleaned the house together on the weekends, a throwback to our early days of marriage when, every Saturday morning, Mando and I would scrub and dust and vacuum all seven hundred square feet of our apartment. They were small steps, but they were significant. I didn't feel alone anymore, inside or outside my home. I was creating a life I didn't want to escape from.

I took a sip of my drink and set the cup back down as I reached for my phone to send a quick text to Mando, letting him know I'd be home in a bit. I decided to window-shop while I enjoyed my coffee. I lingered in the bookstore, admiring cover art and reading book jackets, taking time to be quiet. I bought a book, the latest title from Marisa de los Santos that had come out in May but hadn't yet been added to my collection: *I'll Be Your Blue Sky* had a beautiful spine and would be happy on my shelf.

I stepped into the gift store next door, browsing the water bottles and other practical gifts that sat among items with mild profanity and sarcastic sayings. I bought myself a small green plaque for my desk that read "I used to think I was indecisive but now I'm not sure."

It felt like I was befriending myself, using these gestures to help me shed this deep habit of needing to earn, to prove, to achieve.

I want to be loved for who I am, not what I do, and that had to begin with me.

As I drove home, I thought about these small acts of kindness, the things I would so naturally do for Mando or the boys or for a friend. For too long, I waited for permission to perform these acts for myself. Dr. Cooke gave me a permission slip to quit my job in the spring, but instead, I had amended that permission slip, crossing out what she wrote there.

Now the paper stated I was allowed to carve out space for myself. I had permission to attend to my needs, and I was allowed to do so when I was messy or tired or wonderful or bitchy or just human.

39

NOLAN AND ELI WENT RIGHT to the toddler table when we arrived at the doctor's office. They folded themselves into the absurdly too-small chairs, their knobby knees pointing up to the ceiling, using magnets to move sand around as I checked us in for our appointments with our family PA, Tim—my follow-up, their annuals. I smiled and shook my head and let the good feelings wash over me like a warm wave. I turned my gaze to the trees outside the window, their leaves transformed into tiny red flames in the late-afternoon October sun. Although the interior of the waiting room looked exactly the same as it did when I sat here in the spring, with its muted neutrals and the black-and-white framed prints hanging on the walls, it felt different. I felt different. *Everything changes, and thank God it does.* Finally, I agreed with Kim.

We were all different, it seemed. Mando was improving, and my dad's clean bill of health after his care at Stanford had left me feeling profoundly relieved. He and my mom were boarding a flight to Japan the following morning. The hotel in Tokyo was in need of its general manager, and my parents seemed eager to get back into their routines.

The nurse appeared at the door to the treatment rooms and called my name. "Tim will see you first, and then I'll come get the boys," she said. They nodded a vague acknowledgment, and I followed her.

She pulled the blood pressure cuff tight around my upper arm, and we were both quiet as she inflated it, released the valve, and listened through her stethoscope. She pulled off the cuff with a loud rip of Velcro, noting the results on her clipboard as she asked me to step on the scale. I had managed to gain three pounds over the intervening months.

"Okay." She finished scratching numbers on the paper. "Tim is just finishing up with another patient, and then he'll be right in."

I had just enough time, alone in the room, for a few long exhales and a quiet moment of reflection. I thought back, as I had so many times before, to my last visit with Tim. A quiet knock and then he appeared, rolling his desk ahead of him into the room. After a bit of small talk, Tim asked how it was going with the Zoloft.

"It's good. I feel like it's a sort of safety net. It feels like it's just enough to stop me from worrying that I'll fall too far or too quickly, and that's been huge."

"You seem like you're doing better," he said kindly.

"I am. I feel more like myself," I agreed. "You told me in the spring that wellness was like a wheel, and I realized through the summer that I broke nearly all the spokes at once: I wasn't eating, I wasn't sleeping enough, I wasn't exercising, wasn't doing anything to care for myself. Mando and I returned from the most romantic, magical trip of our lives and then he was suddenly traveling all the time. There's no mystery as to why my mental health fell off the cliff."

"Once we're adults, we sort of think we have it all figured out," Tim explained gently, "and it can be very disorienting to realize we have more growing to do."

"That's so right," I said with a laugh.

Tim asked after my dad, and I briefed him on the latest. "That's great," he said. "He's really lucky."

"I know." I spoke the response with reverence because the words we used—lucky, grateful, relieved—couldn't possibly convey the depth of the feelings behind them.

"And how's Mando?"

"Thanks for asking. He's getting better each week. His physical symptoms are gone now. He doesn't talk about it a lot because he doesn't process things the same way I do, but he's finding good ways to remember his sister. We're framing a picture of Gina and Becky playing the piano—things like that."

"Good. You guys had quite a summer."

"Yes," I said, laughing. "It's been a shitshow."

I felt overwhelmed with gratitude for him. There was more to express about care and trust and the way one person can so greatly affect the life of another, but because I couldn't summon the right words, couldn't say them without crying, I looked him in the eye and said, "Thank you for taking care of us, Tim."

He smiled, knowing the unspoken depth of my gratitude. "You're welcome."

Then the door opened and the kids spilled into the room, all long limbs and happy chaos.

Nolan hopped on the table first. It turned out he had a lot of questions for Tim (there was something to Mando's theory that my loquacious genes were dominant). I sat quietly and tried to be invisible, unobtrusive, wanting both boys to know how to do this without me.

"What's the deal with teenage drinking?" Nolan blurted out the question in the characteristic way of kids his age, their brains simmering with thought until they boil over unexpectedly, questions spilling over the sides. Nolan's fifth-grade DARE program introduced the idea of underage consumption and the middle school health curriculum built on it.

Tim didn't miss a beat. "Well," he began, "when teens drink, they typically drink too much, too fast. They don't know their bodies or their limits, and that makes them more likely to do dangerous things."

This answer satisfied Nolan, and he moved on.

"Why do teenagers do stupid things? Like, with decision-making?"

"The teenage brain will try to trick you. For example," Tim explained, "when I was younger, my teenage brain told me that it was a good idea to ride my bike off a loading dock, when in fact it was a supremely bad idea." We all laughed at this before he continued. "You have to take a moment to step back and think about it from the outside, to ask yourself, *Is this a good idea?*"

Nolan had built up to his final question. "And what happens with teen suicide?"

Children breathe the air of their circumstances. Their sensitive minds and bodies work to filter and make sense of the adult worlds they inhabit. It was a supremely precarious summer. The boys experienced the threat of loss and actual loss; they watched both their parents wade through depression and anxiety. There was no way to measure how their immature selves metabolized the heaviness of that season, and I wondered how it would affect their stories.

"We read about a high-schooler who took his own life recently," I added, giving Tim some context.

Tim nodded slowly. Then he told the boys that sometimes life is hard and that it's normal to feel sad. "But if you find you're having trouble getting out of that sadness, or if you're having thoughts that tell you it's never going to get better, that's when you need to open up your mouth and start talking."

I wanted to gather the moment into my arms and hold it close and savor it. The antiseptic smell and the other goofy boy questions and the awkward, open beauty that materialized there in that exam room—it was all supremely beautiful to me. These were, again, good old days. I was witnessing truth make its way to my boys through someone else, which made it more precious. I didn't have to engineer this lesson like a manic puppeteer. My boys were approaching the age when they would begin to live their own stories, when their lives would crowd with more influences and truth tellers until magically, one day in the future, they would grow into who they were meant to become. It would have less to do with me than I had previously imagined, which was strange and freeing.

I was their everything for a season, but seasons change. The leaves were dropping from the trees and the days were growing shorter, but on that day I was finally able to appreciate the autumn colors instead of worrying about the chill of winter. I rested in the knowledge that even if I were gone, there would be people who would love my boys and shape their lives.

To say I felt lucky didn't cover it.

After the doctor's office, we went to In-N-Out for a milkshake and sat in the drive-thru line with the windows down to let the cool breeze flow through the car. As we wound our way around the exterior of the restaurant, I said to them, "Guys, you know what Tim was saying about opening your mouth if you need help? That's exactly what I've done this summer, and it's what I do when I go see Kim."

"We know, Mom," Eli said gently, speaking for both of them.

"I want you to know that there's always a way through. Sometimes you have to try a few doors before you find it." I told them that, before seeing Tim, I'd seen another doctor, my gynecologist, and she'd told me to quit my job.

"Why did she do that?" Nolan inquired.

"Well, I think she didn't know me, so she gave advice that she felt was right. But it wasn't right for me, and thankfully, I figured that out. Then I talked to Tim. But the important piece is that I started talking. Don't ever be afraid to ask for support, from me or Dad or someone we trust, like Tim, or even Kim."

I flicked my eyes up to the rearview mirror and saw the boys' slightly glazed eyes, an indication that they were only halfway listening to my hard-earned mom wisdom. Ungrateful turds.

"Or you can find a stranger, preferably one with a van who offers you candy, and ask the creepy stranger for help," I continued.

Nolan snapped up his head to make eye contact with me in

the mirror before he said in a shocked tone, "What? Why would we do that?"

I cackled a little and they started to laugh, getting the joke. "Just wanted to make sure you were listening, pal."

Mando made salmon for my parents that evening, their last dinner stateside. We marked the close of a chapter. None of us would be sad to turn this particular page.

I glanced at my dad across the table. He looked good. His cheeks were pink, and he smiled at the boys, listening indulgently as they described video games and LEGO sets in exhaustive detail. My mom gazed at her grandsons and her husband with heart-bursting tenderness. Someone suggested a family game of Bullshit, and the boys popped up from the table to grab cards, knowing they'd be exempt from clearing the table tonight. Grandparents make it rain privileges, and they were taking full advantage.

The boys plopped down on the floor next to the coffee table, and my parents sat on the couch across from them. They shuffled and dealt the cards while I pulled dishes from the table, scraping plates and inverting glasses to place them in the dishwasher. They were giggling before they started the game.

I listened to the boys laugh as Mando came over to dry the dishes next to me, smiling at the joy of the scene playing out around the coffee table. He put his hand on my waist and pulled me to him as I leaned my head onto his shoulder. He tipped his head onto mine and we stayed like that for a beat, bound together by chores and children and family and hearts that pump oxygen and blood and love without obstruction.

40

MY THIRTY-NINTH BIRTHDAY FELL on a Tuesday. The crisp November morning air bit my cheeks as I rode my bike to work, making them slightly rosy by the time I arrived at the school.

When I first returned to the library, I tiptoed through the days as if I were crossing a recently frozen lake in early winter. I weighed every choice, every step, constantly examining my moods, my body, and my thoughts before picking up each foot and gingerly replacing it on the ice. It seemed too thin to support my weight, and I would sometimes stand completely still, listening intently for the crack that would precede my crash into the freezing water. But the sound didn't come, and I'd exhale in relief and take another step. With each footfall, I grew more confident, and then I was walking, not quickly or jubilantly, but steadily. Occasionally I feared the inevitable sound of a small crack, but it no longer elicited heart-stopping panic. Sometimes I didn't even slow down to investigate.

It had been ten weeks of average, ten weeks of adequate, ten weeks of focusing on the parts of the job that brought me the most joy. And everything had been fine—often better than fine.

That morning, I greeted my coworkers in the front office as I made my way to the library. Waiting for my computer to boot up, I checked in the small number of books that I found in the return bin, sliding each book under the bright red light of the scanner until I heard the beep and saw the title pop up on the monitor. Then, I responded to emails until the class of first-graders paraded past my desk to seat themselves in the squares on the rainbow carpet, their teacher issuing quiet instructions as they arranged themselves. I stood and walked around the edge of my desk, carrying a copy of *Miss Nelson Is Missing!* in my right hand.

"Friends," the teacher prompted, "are we ready?"

Twenty-four first-grade faces turned their attention from her to me. Then she led them in a round of "Happy Birthday." I soaked in the serenade, loving their enthusiastic, high-pitched, off-key voices.

"Wow, guys," I said when they were finished, "you sure know how to make me feel special." They grinned, satisfied with their efforts. We read about Miss Viola Swamp, and I was there for every word: present, whole, and supremely grateful to be so.

I collected smiles and birthday wishes throughout the day as the rest of the classes passed through the library. Some brought cards written with fat, scented Mr. Sketch markers. Some looked me in the eye after I checked out their books and wished me a happy birthday. All the kind gestures were shared with an uncomplicated, forthright sweetness.

Later that night, after dinner, Mando opened a bottle from Ruinart, one of the champagne houses we visited in France. It was decadent and perfect and I smiled, both at his thoughtfulness and at the memory. He turned the label toward me before pouring it into two flutes, the bubbles rising happily as he passed me the glass. Nolan pulled the carton of milk out of the refrigerator and poured a glass for himself and his brother, while Eli grabbed a white bakery box and removed a small chocolate cake. Mando placed three candles into the cake and lit them, and then he slid the plate toward me as he and the boys sang the most precious "Happy Birthday" I'd heard all day.

My boys' faces were illuminated by the candles, the soft glow reflecting in their dark eyes, and I felt happy. But more important, I felt grounded. I was rooted in my life, in the day, in these people who loved and knew me.

Everything changes. But on that day, I had all of this, and it was far more than enough.

41

LITTLE BY LITTLE: IT'S THE heartbeat of any recovery. You begin by believing the people who love you, who assure you it can—it will—get better. The process is brutal and grueling and slower than you would like, but you keep going, little by little, until one day you realize each step doesn't require unimaginable effort. And after that, you find the rhythm again. And then you start the next season, the next story. You move forward into a new, unknowable future. But you keep the joy and wisdom and resilience you've earned with your pain and grit. The gifts of the recovery are yours to keep.

I walked through the holidays in just this manner: little by little. Kim continued to ask me the right questions, and in doing so, she handed me new tools. They felt too heavy in my hand at first, but after a few uses, their handles formed to my grip, and I was able to wield them with competence and, sometimes, even confidence. I was continuing to learn to say yes to what gave me joy and no to a whole host of obligations I really, really didn't want to do. Of course I occasionally reverted to persistent, pesky old habits—predicting disaster or diagnosing myself with psychological disorders and allergies or agreeing to something that clearly should've been a no. But I learned to be gentle with myself, to take my own hand and distract myself as if I were an overtired toddler, saying gently, "Let's do something else." Little by little, I found the beat again.

I had an appointment with Kim in late March. I commented on her new clock, told her about some neighborhood gossip. Even after two weeks, I didn't have much to address. We were just catching up. We may as well have had a plate of small cucumber sandwiches between us, dainty cups of tea in our hands.

"Kim, thank you for all you've done for me. You're very good at what you do."

"I appreciate that," she said sincerely, "but it's because we're a good fit for each other. You're insightful by nature, but I'm able to help you think about things a little differently."

I was very fortunate that Kim and I had clicked, that she had been able to see past the fragile woman on the couch to a more whole version of me. She believed we could resurrect that woman. She believed it for both of us.

I looked up at Kim. Her hair was down and behaving well, as usual. I looked at her familiar, comforting face and then glanced at the clock to see we were nearly out of time.

I felt a brief stab of hesitation, a reflexive jerk of *I don't really like change*, before I took a deep breath and plunged ahead. "Is it okay if I call you or text you when I'm ready for my next appointment?" I knew this was the natural and right and expected next step, but the words hung between us, and I felt the tiniest pinch of grief between my eyes, the slight sting of tears. Everything changes, and sometimes I still hated it.

But I felt better when I glanced up to see Kim smiling. She nodded encouragingly, as if I had pegged the right answer, and said, "That sounds perfect."

Shay and I sat together at the small round conference table in her office as we reviewed the printed form for my annual review. She gave me positive feedback. In addition to updating the library's books on technology (the one with a typewriter on the cover really had to go), I'd begun hosting lunchtime book clubs with the easy, straightforward goal of enjoying books with the fifth-graders. It turned out my work had been more than adequate.

We finished the formalities and both signed the piece of paper that sat between us before she leaned back slightly in her chair. I looked up at her and said, "Thank you, Shay. Thank you for helping me figure out how to keep going with this job. I'm truly grateful." When I'd walked into her office in the spring, she'd validated the difficulty of balancing work and motherhood. She had helped me feel less alone.

"Of course," she said genuinely. "We wanted to keep you, Julie."

I can't say if what had happened to me was avoidable. When I returned to work, I received plenty of general advice about "letting things slide," but no one could define precisely what those "things" were. Burnout crept up on me quickly and quietly, as it does for many women.

Once the scales were tipped, it was extremely difficult to rebalance them. Our medical system doesn't provide a soft landing for those who need support with their mental health. I have yet to see a box on any form for Mom Experiencing Extreme Burnout. I was an educated, driven woman with resources, and I struggled to find support in those early weeks when I knew something was wrong but couldn't seem to articulate what it was. What about those who don't have my advantages or resources or knowledge of the system? It would be so easy to fall through the cracks or to muddle along in a sad, persistent autopilot state.

"It's hard for women to keep themselves on the to-do list," I told Shay. "The world asks a lot, doesn't it?"

Shay nodded, and then we stood up together. "You should write a book about that," she said, as I headed for the door.

EPILOGUE

THREE YEARS HAD PASSED SINCE The Night I Couldn't Turn Off the Lights. I lay on the couch on a Saturday afternoon in June reading *Malibu Rising,* a book I'd eagerly anticipated since reading *The Seven Husbands of Evelyn Hugo* and subsequently recommending it to every person I knew. There was laundry to be done. We had managed the worst of COVID, but it had far from disappeared. Nolan was about to start high school and had already joined the cross-country team. I hadn't even known he could run, and now he was huffing and puffing through Pleasanton for hours on end. Eli was playing the saxophone, like his dad, and he was beginning to get good at it. In the outside world, things were undoubtedly precarious—but I only occasionally felt precarious, which was a gift that hadn't lost its luster.

Nolan walked by into the kitchen to scrounge for food in the refrigerator. His back faced me as he peered into the lighted interior like it was a crystal ball that would tell him how to satisfy his unbelievable teen-boy hunger. He was six feet tall, which was especially strange because he still felt like my baby. His muscles were defined from his early forays into athletics, which annoyed Mando to no end. Mando was sweating like a farm animal while working out in the hot garage to stave off the dreaded middle-age paunch, and here was Nolan, rolling around the house in a towel, eating constantly, and somehow sporting a six-pack.

Mando walked into the kitchen and barked at Nolan, "Shut the fridge. You're wasting energy." Mando has a thing about energy, whereas I sometimes leave the TV on all day because I like to come home and see it on, especially when Mando is traveling. Sorry, environment. I am trying to use less plastic, if that helps.

I shook my head and returned my eyes to the pages of my book as Nolan and Mando bickered about the fact that Nolan "should think about what he wants to eat before opening the fridge." Eli wandered into the room and then back out again, having the second-child sense to understand that he should wait on any requests for the moment. He'd come back for cereal after Dad was gone.

I simply kept reading. I used to jump up like I was in a game of Whac-A-Mole, attending to everyone's needs: soothing, feeding, deciding to put in a load of laundry while I was up. But I didn't do that as much anymore. I attended to my own needs.

Nolan sauntered over, chomping on an apple.

"Mom."

"Yes?" I said it without looking up.

"I have a question." He took a bite of his apple and stood next to me, trying to read over my shoulder. I pushed him away, and he smirked, knowing I hate it when he crowds me.

I slid my finger in to mark my page and looked straight at him, beaming a beatific smile before saying, "Sweetie, go ask your dad."

He rolled his eyes and took another bite of his apple before wandering off. He probably didn't even have a question.

It was a tiny act, this leave-me-alone-I'm-reading interaction, but I had learned the tiny acts matter, and had embraced a slow process of little adjustments. These small, intentional acts paved the way through, the way back. After too long caring for everyone but myself, I had learned to care for everyone *and* myself.

Eli walked over to give me a kiss on the head. Nolan moved through the room to answer his pinging cell phone. He informed me that he was leaving to meet a friend at the neighborhood park and came over to give me a hug and say goodbye. Mando made me an afternoon coffee in the new espresso machine I bought (which he bitched about but then later admitted was the best money we'd ever spent and I was right and he was wrong). He set the small cup on the end table, and I thanked him.

Tiny acts of love, offered to me by my closest, most precious people who are positioned at the center of a wider circle. These people, those people, and even me: our tiny acts make my story beautiful.

In fact, they make my story perfect.

ACKNOWLEDGMENTS

I HAVE LOVED WATCHING THIS book come to life.

I've been fortunate to work with a parade of talented editors who have ushered me forward. Thank you to Brooke Warner, who was the first person to help me believe I could become an author. Brooke, thank you for teaching me about memoir. I'm beyond grateful for you and She Writes Press. Jordan Blumetti, thank you for helping me settle into my groove as a writer and embrace the joy of being funny on the page. Pam Cannon, thank you for giving me tools and perspective at key moments. And Bridie Loverro, you helped me transform the final drafts with your intention, understanding, and loving attention. Thank you.

To the Zibby Books team: so many of you have become friends. Thank you for the care you've shown me and this book. And thank you for giving me your cell phone numbers so that I could text you a lot and then call you on the old-fashioned phone anyway.

ACKNOWLEDGMENTS

Special thanks to Chelsea Grogan for teaching me about spreadsheets and running and being a dynamite producer for *Ask a Librarian,* and to Sherri Puzey for her unfailing belief in me and this story. Kathleen, I like you so much I'm not even annoyed I had to revise these acknowledgements. And Zibby, I love your heart for books and authors. Thank you for your drive, your warmth, and for inviting me to publish my book with you. To say it's a dream come true is an understatement.

Graça Tito, thank you for designing a cover that feels so much like me, and Anne Messitte, thank you for helping create the gorgeous interior.

I treasure my relationships with the other authors at Zibby Books. Jane and Michelle, I adore you and think you're both very photogenic.

To my agent, Naomi Eisenbeiss at InkWell Management: you've been one of the most delightful surprises in this journey. Working with you is a joy.

To Courtney Maum, Anna Whiston-Donaldson, Stephanie Thornton Plymale, and Abby Maslin: the measure of a person is the way they treat someone from whom they have nothing to gain. Thank you for taking time to read and blurb the first form of this book. I held your words of encouragement close to my heart throughout the process.

To Joanna Rakoff, Rebecca Pacheco, and every other author who befriended me along the way: thank you for welcoming me into a club of fierce, lovely, talented writers. Your presence has multiplied the joy.

Kim Olson, you're a healer. Thank you for seeing past the shell of a woman on your couch and for believing I could find my way back to myself. I'm so glad we could spend the last few years learning about book publishing together.

Mom and Dad, I'm incredibly blessed to be your daughter. Thank you for loving me so well. Brian, thank you for being my first friend in life and for quoting the right movies with me at all times. Amy, you're my best sister, and I whole love you.

I'm fortunate to be known and loved by my friends, only a few of whom are named in this book. Allie, April, Jess, Kristin, Cathie, Lori, Keely, Adrienne, Margo, Emily: your hearts are tied to mine. You and your families make our life beautiful.

Every person at Fairlands Elementary is part of this dream (including my small friends, who believe in me without a second thought). Kalli, Lisa, Kelly, Kaycie, Katie, Jenny, Heidi, Alison, Shay, Kelley: to be loved so well at the place where I work is a tremendous gift. I adore sharing my days with you, even though the children really seem to need a lot and it gets in the way of our conversations.

Eli and Nolan, I love being your mom. It really is my favorite job. Watching you grow into young men is one of the great privileges of my life. Thank you for supporting me as I wrote this book—for loving me, for believing I could do it, and for being so kind and good and funny. I love you 3000.

Mando, as I wrote this book, I felt completely free to write about us and our lives: the good, the bad, the arguing in the airport. Thank you for all you've done to make this dream possible. I love you, and I love our life together. I can't wait to see what movie is on TV tonight.

ABOUT THE AUTHOR

JULIE CHAVEZ is an elementary school librarian in Northern California. Though thousands of books pass through her hands each month, *Everyone But Myself* is the first one written by her. Julie lives with her husband and two tall teenagers in a house where she arranges her books by color.

⦿ @juliewriteswords
www.juliewriteswords.com